Other books by the same author:

In course of preparation:

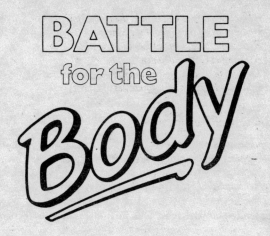

BATTLE for the Body

Hugh B. Black

NEW DAWN BOOKS

GREENOCK, SCOTLAND

© Hugh B. Black 1988

First published 1988 by
NEW DAWN BOOKS
27 Denholm Street, Greenock PA16 8RH, Scotland

ISBN 1 870944 05 4

Extended biblical quotations are from the Revised Version

Cover photo: Craig Richardson

Production and printing in England for
NEW DAWN BOOKS
27 Denholm Street, Greenock PA16 8RH, Scotland
by Nuprint Ltd, Harpenden, Herts AL5 4SE

Contents

Acknowledgements

I am grateful to all those who continue to encourage me to write; to my wife Isobel and to my daughter Dr Alison H. Black for editorial assistance; to Miss Pauline Anderson, Mr Alastair Duff and Miss Jennifer Jack for proof-reading and helpful advice; to Miss Ina Thomson and Alison for transcribing the basic text from tape recordings; and to Miss Irene Morrison for laborious work in processing the various drafts of the book.

Foreword

It is appropriate that this book should be written for these times.

In many Christian circles revival is discussed with increasing regularity and an ever-deepening sense of expectation. I believe that revival has to begin first of all in individual Christian lives with each believer walking in righteousness and living daily in victory by the power of the indwelling Spirit, and then the Church, which is His Body, will be ready for the Lord's return.

There is no question that this book will be mightily used to prepare the born-again believer for the great time of harvest. The contents will challenge and encourage you and, if you are prepared, could change your Christian walk. You will find its pages useful for reference, particularly when you feel that the enemy is gaining the upper hand in your own spiritual battle.

The book's title is very appropriate. Frequently in the New Testament the Christian life is likened to a battle and the author, in his own inimitable fashion, clearly shows in these pages where the battle will rage, at the hottest points. I am sure that this book will help you to become an overcomer in the battle for your soul, and then you too, like St. Paul, will be able to say, 'Thanks be to God Who in Christ always leads us in triumph.'

Finally, might I say how pleased I am that part two has been devoted to the testimony of Johnnie Hamilton, as it was under his ministry that I came into the Baptism in the Holy Spirit, and it was Johnnie's ministry that the Lord used to bring my brother and father to the place of salvation.

Drew Greenwood

Preface

As in ordinary battles rival commanders aim for the same strategic points and seek to exploit each other's weaknesses, so in the spiritual war, where the bodies of men are the battlefield, God and Satan aim to secure control of the same vital centres. Each is interested in areas of weakness—Satan that he may enter and destroy—God that He may guard and strengthen. Satan wants the body to be under his control, obeying his commands and ultimately being possessed by him. God wants the same body that it may be wholly His—a channel for His Spirit; holy, strong and pure.

Part one of this book deals with the following strategic parts of the body: the head, eyes, ears, tongue, shoulders, heart, knees, backbone, hands, feet (including the Achilles tendon) and finally the reproductive organs. It is based on a series of sermons preached in August 1986 at a conference in Scotland. The sermons have been adapted for publication and a final chapter added.

As I indicated in my preface to *Consider Him* I am aware that there is a great difference between spoken and written English. I trust the work will not lose too much as a result of its origin.

Part two contains the testimony of the Rev John Hamilton. This has intrigued thousands of people in Britain, Europe, India and America over recent years. It speaks of the plight of man and the power of God, of human depravity and Divine Grace. The story has in it a compelling power and throws light on the unusual ministry in which Mr Hamilton is now used.

As I indicated in an earlier work, I have been encouraged to include testimonies in my books. In this case I am reminded of the story of the man and the camel out in the desert. A sand-storm arose and the man was sorry for the poor camel and thought he should at least allow it to put its head inside the tent. He did, and fell asleep. In the morning he wakened up outside the tent with the camel inside.

Far be it from me to suggest that Mr Hamilton is like the camel out in the sand-storm or that he tried to come into this book. I approached him and asked if I might put his story together from tapes I had taken. As I have watched the pages come off the word processor I have felt, however, that the camel is taking over the tent—but it really is a very interesting camel!

I have deliberately done little editing. Johnnie's style is quite unique. His preaching is colloquial and colourful and I felt his testimony would lose much of its impact if I tried to put it into a Shakespearean mould—even if I had been fit for such an undertaking! I trust you will enjoy reading the story as much as I have enjoyed 'hearing' it again.

PART 1

BATTLE FOR THE BODY

1

Drawing up the Battle Lines

Recently I have been reading two biographies: one on General Montgomery of Alamein fame and the other on Montrose.

Both of these men were outstanding generals in their day and amongst the greatest in our history. Montrose was evidently a master of both strategy and tactics and his battles, although involving comparatively small numbers, showed his genius. Of Montgomery it has been said that prior to Alamein we had no victories and after Alamein we suffered no defeats.

As I pondered the text, 'Your adversary the devil goeth about as a roaring lion seeking whom he may devour,' there came back to mind some of the things I learned in reading those biographies. When these men went into battle there were two thoughts in their minds—the thought of victory and the thought of defeat—their victory and their enemy's defeat. While Montgomery was concentrating on the defeat of Rommel, Rommel for his part was concentrating on the defeat of Montgomery. There they were, pitted against each other; the battle lines were drawn and the hour of engagement came. And I suddenly realised that in a deeper, sterner, more awful battle there comes the hour of engagement and the opposing commanders are in position. For ever there is God opposing Satan and Satan opposing God.

There can be times of skirmishing around but there comes a time like the present when we are gathered for spiritual purposes. Some may look on Camp time as holiday time, but there are others who look on it as a time supremely for battle—a time for war—a time when the preparations have been made and the troops are ready for action. Such an hour is this. I know that while in the natural world men and women may be thinking of holiday, in the spiritual world Satan is planning war and God also is going to war, and whether you like it or not you will be caught up in this war. There were many camp followers in bygone days who only wanted to be camp followers but again and again they were caught up in war: again and again they were massacred. They were involved whether they liked it or not, whether they wanted to go to war or not. It was a time of war. It was a time of engagement.

I have noticed also that no-one is the same after battle. You'll find that ground is either gained or lost. If you lose ground you can become discouraged and disillusioned and more vulnerable to further attack, and if you gain ground you can preserve and consolidate your gain and become stronger to resist further attack. This is vital and very important. We are not merely looking for good meetings for a week. We are looking for changes to be wrought in lives —changes that will be permanent. We want ground to be secured and not lost again.

The North African campaign prior to Montgomery's day was very like many Christian lives. The armies went back and forward across North Africa—the British chasing the Italians and the Germans chasing and being chased by the British. They went backward and forward but there came a time when Montgomery ended this. He did not merely want to chase the enemy but he wanted to secure the land and to prevent their return. To this end he wanted to destroy. He had no fancy words about this. I'm just telling you what his attitude was. He told his soldiers bluntly, 'You are here to kill the enemy, not just to take ground. You are here to kill—to destroy.' That was the attitude of war— that was the attitude of battle. Now you might have a nice namby-pamby attitude to your engagement with Satan but I tell you he has no nice namby-pamby attitude towards you. His objective is to take souls captive, to destroy souls. 'Your enemy the devil goeth about as a roaring lion seeking whom he may devour.' This is his objective.

Let us ponder a little longer on our military analogy. There are generals who have been very famous and have had their victories who tell us very little about their thinking, but Montgomery wasn't like that. He spoke openly and made his views and principles very plain. Indeed he put them in black and white and his basic thinking became apparent. His attitude wasn't casual. It wasn't floppy. It was clearly defined and he had a set purpose. I think that Montrose probably had exactly the same type of approach.

I would like to give you the kind of picture that I have in my mind. Suppose yourself to be in command of an army with an opposing force coming against you: how would you arrange your forces? If theirs is a strong force will you try for balance, equal force against force, and will you attack evenly all along the line? That is not how the big commanders think at all. Montgomery would have looked for a weak spot and he would have brought devastating force against that point so that he might destroy and blast a hole right through the enemy line, and then quickly have encircling movements to contain and destroy what he had encircled. A blast through on the point of weakness! That is what Satan is minded to do to you—to look for your point of weakness and bring against that point devastating force so that he may cripple and destroy. That is Satanic strategy.

So if, in your army, you had a weak point and you were a skilful commander, what would you do if you had time for preparation? I'll tell you what these two commanders did. They immediately searched out such points in their own armies. Montgomery was ruthless, absolutely ruthless. He could take up a new command and within about twenty-four hours he might have sacked one or two brigadiers, one or two majors, ten captains, and rooted out a fair number of his officers and told them in more or less unkind words they were useless and should go home, that they were menaces and should never have been where they were. They were unfitted for command. He might initially ask one or two leading questions and discover that, by his standards, they were not up to their jobs. If you had challenged him on the severity of his actions he would have said, 'We are dealing with the lives of men. War is not a game. I cannot *afford* to have inefficiency in my army and I will *not* have inefficiency in my army.' He was very particular about authority too. Former commanders of the Eighth Army seem to have been gentlemanly in their approach to their officers and allowed some measure of debate on orders. Montgomery posted a terse message, 'My orders are given to be obeyed—not to form a basis for discussion.' He was also liable to say and indeed did say, 'You must all be in the peak of physical condition, for which purpose you'll do a seven-mile run each morning before breakfast—officers and men.' On one memorable occasion a tubby colonel didn't want to run for seven miles (and I don't blame him) and came to Montgomery with a medical certificate, a smile in his eye, and said, 'You know it would be dangerous for me to run. I'm liable to drop dead with a heart attack.' Poor colonel! Montgomery said, 'It would be much better to do so on a run than in the height of a battle where you would endanger other men's lives. You run!' It was a case of either running there or running home. He ran and he didn't have a heart attack.

Have you got the point? Montgomery looked for the areas of weakness and dealt with them and if he discovered that his men were not well drilled he dealt with the matter. If their training was deficient he attended to it. Soon almost every soldier under his command became a crack soldier and every company a crack company, highly trained and disciplined and acting as an integrated part of the whole army. All the points of weakness had been taken into account.

I want you to know tonight that there are two mighty commanders in spiritual warfare—God and Satan. Yes, Satan too is a mighty commander but you have a mightier Lord. They are both concentrating in this week on your points of weakness: Satan that he may come in devastating power and destroy; God that he may come and strengthen you on your point of weakness that you may become strong to do battle with Satan and overcome in hours of temptation and trial. As you strengthen you will gain ground and Satan's power will weaken where these areas are concerned. So they are both coming, and if there is one point in your life that you do not want touched it is likely to be your point of weakness. That's the point you don't want anybody to talk about, you don't want anybody to think about and you don't want to think about it yourself. You don't want it exposed.

I was born on a farm and as a child had a very strict upbringing. On one occasion one of the workers tried to teach me to smoke. I would be about four or five at the time. Now my father had a particularly strict attitude about anything like that. He was a very kind man but on this occasion he said, 'If you want to smoke I'll burn your nose and you'll get all the smoke you'll ever need!' I got caught with a cigarette. To tell you the truth I never really did have a smoke. I puffed in the wrong direction but I had the thing in my hand and I was caught. I remember the family gathered round and I felt so very small—I wanted to hide; I wanted to go away. About thirty years later one of my daughters was caught as a child doing something similarly forbidden. I remember her saying, 'I don't want to talk about that. I want to go away.' It brought back my own case vividly. The hidden thing you don't want touched. You don't want anybody to explore that one thing—and do you know, that is the one thing that God will touch and the one thing on which Satan will fight. You are in the centre position and if you go Satan's way you can go crashing down, and it is a dangerous thing to go crashing down in a time when God is minded to bless. If you stand your ground and resist Satan he will flee and you will grow stronger. You will find that you will take ground and that the gain can be permanent.

I am not talking in vague, theoretic terms. I've been in this kind of work now for a long time and we are told not to be ignorant of Satan's devices. He has devices and even although one knows this, one is quite often caught and I was nearly caught today. In coming here we had been held up for about three hours in a traffic jam and that maybe wasn't a good beginning, although I'm a reasonably patient person (actually I fell asleep in the middle of it). I didn't really feel particularly ruffled at that point but suddenly something struck me. I suspected one of my daughters of misdemeanour and it annoyed me. It really did annoy me, and the more I thought about it the more annoyed I became. She's not perfect, you know! Now God didn't actually say (though He might have done!) that I wasn't perfect either. Suddenly I realised I was becoming unnaturally irritated and I saw a red light. The thing in itself wasn't a major matter and I hadn't even proved her guilty: I was only suspicious. But I became aware of an irrational irritation creeping over my spirit which was going to disturb my relationship with Christ—and I saw and smelt the enemy and I said, 'No! No!' and refused to give way to something that would have been very wrong indeed.

There are times when you are allowed to be angry. There is a word which says, 'Be angry and sin not. Let not the sun go down upon your wrath.' I was very angry last night on quite a different issue and again the longer I thought about the matter that angered me the angrier I became and I had no bad conscience about it at all. Indeed I had rather a slight regret that I hadn't got really angry quicker!

I had been in my car with one of my brothers and we were behind a lady driver as we approached traffic lights. The stream of traffic on my right was approaching the same light and one car which was just a little ahead of us drew abreast of the lady driver. There were four or five young fools in the car and two of them put down their windows and began to shout abuse at the lady—not about her driving, but just sexual insults, and that lady was alone in her car. I was livid but my anger didn't rise quickly enough because if it had done I would have been quite capable of pursuing that car with my hand on the horn and blasting them from Greenock to Glasgow to draw the attention of the police. I was absolutely enraged that that could happen to a lady. It can be quite dangerous when you get a group of young fellows like that. They can sometimes make things very awkward for ladies driving alone. The more I thought about it the angrier I became. Now I had no bad conscience about that, none at all. If it was happening out there right now I could go out and pursue them without any feeling of breaking communion with Christ. I don't think we should be soft or stand by when that kind of thing is happening, but the other case in which I was irritated was quite different. There was a different feeling. There was selfishness in it and there was

21

something wrong.

In a time like this Conference, as God draws near, watch for small irritations, small annoyances. Watch that the habits of those with whom you are sharing accommodation don't get on your nerves to the point of disturbing your spiritual life (and watch that your habits don't get on their nerves!). Put all these things aside that you might know Christ; leave your life as an open book for God to come and reveal what He wants done this week. Resist the devil, who may well try to stir you to the point where you want to go away home. It's normal for quite a number of people to want to go home on the first day or two, so if you have that feeling take it from me you are likely to be a real sinner— that is often a sure sign that you, maybe above all others, need to stay! If you have that awful urge to run for it, there may even be a demon there. Demons frequently want to run when the power of God becomes strong in the midst of a community. I am aware, of course, that these remarks will inhibit any of you who may be tempted to go!

Now let me say this. There were times when Montgomery was in danger of defeat and it was 'a close-run thing' as Wellington could say on another occasion. There were times when Montrose was defeated although he was a great general; sometimes the odds were very great against him, but I have to tell you that our General is never defeated and you will never be defeated when you obey His commands. Victory is assured. The devil cannot win if we obey God. Supposing the odds are stacked against you one hundred to one, the devil won't win if you obey your Commander. Ponder that. God will look for your places of weakness and make you strong men and women. Satan will look for these same places to destroy you. You can have victory if you want it. It's as simple as that; but you have to want it. You have to want Him more than all on earth beside. It is over to you.

2

The Mind

Those of you who were here at the last Camp in July will remember that on the mornings I took a series of ten studies on qualities of Christ: Peace and Serenity; Purity and Tranquillity; Love and Compassion; Strength and Courage; Self-effacement and God-centredness.[1] For this Camp nothing really opened until after the service last night. Then, as you know, I spoke on spiritual warfare, battlefield strategy, tactics, and the fact that there were two commanders—God Himself on one side, and the wicked one on the other. I indicated that there was conflict between the two, and that a Camp time was normally a time of very particular engagement when the battle is fought over and in men and women. The opposing commanders are both interested in the strategic points within a personality and they are also interested in the weak points, the areas of vulnerability. Much of the battle is fought in and over the body and the first part of the body on which I want to concentrate this morning is the head.

You may say, 'I never thought of the head as being an area of weakness.' Well, it is, in fact, one of the areas of greatest weakness and it is the one that receives perhaps the greatest attention from the rival commanders. I want you to remember the word that says 'the whole world lieth in the wicked one' and that you have been in what you might call enemy territory: that Satan has a fearful grip on the human race. But you are not totally in his hand—the land is not totally taken over by him. And there are areas that God is fighting to reclaim. Once the land all belonged to God, but with sin there came a curse upon a fair creation. Don't for one moment think that you start on level terms: equally God's and Satan's. Remember the word, 'the whole world lieth in the wicked one'. The Fall has brought a shadow, a curse upon our faculties, upon our minds, upon our hearts, upon our spirits. From the very beginning there is a dark shadow. There is in us a predisposition to be evil and to do evil. Make no mistake about this kind of thing. Don't be taken in with the idea that man is wonderful and is getting better and better every day. Man is wicked. He is shapen in iniquity. He is born in sin. He is born a lost, hell-deserving creature. What does the Word say? 'There is none good.' 'We have all fallen short of the glory of God.' As seen by a Holy God we are depraved. We are corrupt.

You say, 'I don't believe it.' No, indeed, if you are dwelling in the midst of it you may not recognise it, but if for one moment you could see humanity through Divine eyes you would be appalled at the depth of human corruption and human sin.

I remember hearing of one of the early Pentecostal teachers in Britain who at the time of his Baptism in the Spirit was out of the body for many hours. He evidently had visions of both Heaven and hell. In the first he was shown the crown room. There were crowns of various shapes and sizes but there was one more beautiful than all the others and he spoke of it to his guide in glowing terms, to be told that that particular crown was for him and that everybody felt the same about his own particular crown. He was shown

a room full of crosses and there was one repulsive above all
the others. When he was laid upon it he was pained at every
part of his body. Any other cross would have been preferable
to that one. It was made clear to him that his own cross was
peculiarly fitted for him (as our crosses always are) and to
evade the cross meant losing the crown.

The scene moved to the battlements of Heaven from
where he looked down to earth. There rose from men an
almost intolerable stench. It was fearful in the pure air of
Heaven. Indication was then given that he was to go back
down and he desperately did not want to go. He was then
shown the Cross with Christ again upon it and he was asked
if for His sake he would go. Willingly he agreed and he
awakened back in the body. A wonderful vision—but note
the point of the story in this context. He had lived on earth
and never known how horrible the stench of sin really
was—he had never known it until he breathed the pure air
of Heaven. He had never known it until he felt with the
feeling of God Himself.

Pigs, you realise, aren't upset by their own smell; they are
making it and they are living in it. It is clinging to them, but
you go into a piggery that hasn't been cleaned out for a week
and you'll find it intolerable. Now we live in the midst of sin
and we are sinners by nature and practice and often scarcely
notice our condition. Things that would have a shattering
effect in the Glory land are with us on our right hand and on
our left and we scarcely notice. So don't get any false ideas
about our beauty and our goodness. In our nature we are
fallen. We are born deformed and twisted and if we realise
this from the beginning it can make things a great deal
easier for us. God moved in Christ to redeem men and
Christ paid the ransom for our sins on Calvary and He
brings us back to Himself, but in many ways we are still
gripped by that wicked one and God goes to war against him
to set us free. Satan attacks strategic points and weak points.

The first of these I want to consider this morning is the Mind. I want you to see homo sapiens in the central place, with God on the right hand and Satan on the left hand. Satan has our ear. He has had it for years. He disguises his voice and he comes along and says, 'You have a good mind.' Oh, don't we like to hear that? 'Yes, that's right. That is a nice thought. Yes. I do have a good mind. When I think of how stupid some other people are I do seem to have a good mind.' Satan goes on, 'You know you were given your mind to think with. Now one thing you should be careful about is to keep an independent mind. That is important. Keep an independent mind.' Isn't it true that when you went to school you were taught the same thing—'think for yourself, young fellow—do your own thinking'. It is drilled in from early stages: I did it myself many a time. Oh yes, yes...and those of you who have studied in the lower, and the middle, and the higher reaches of education, will know that while you are supposed to think for yourselves woe betide you if you do too much of it!

A great tragedy befell one of you recently. One young man who has quite an independent mind, in the good sense of that word, discovered that he could write a very acceptable essay—a real shrewd Scottish kind of essay. In this he portrayed a man out walking with his companion. There ensued a good deal of talk with his companion and then, at the end, came the twist. The companion turned out to be a dog. This gave the essay a lovely turn and the young man got high credit for this piece of work when he first submitted it. This was original and independent thought. This was good. Indeed it was so good that his teacher read it out to the class and a number of others also thought it a good idea. Now Stephen, the essayist, being a sharp boy and having been given a good mark for the essay on one occasion, used it again on another suitable occasion with another teacher. It became known as 'the dog essay'. When, however, a number of others cottoned on to the idea and produced I don't know how many dog essays, things changed!

The marker who sits down to mark an original essay gives it high credit but after he marks half a dozen other essays, all of which are dog essays, he becomes very suspicious. Has the teacher taught this? The marks he then assigns are very low.

You see you get credit for independent thought and you are taught to think independently. I remember in my own University days we were studying Anglo-Saxon history, which was a difficult field. There was one particularly difficult textbook by Jolliffe. I don't know whether the younger generation reading History now still meet him, but his English was very difficult to follow. It was convoluted. I remember my lecturer saying, 'Oh, but there's meat in Jolliffe. There's meat in Jolliffe.' But the problem lay in getting the meat out. Now there was another scholar who had produced a wonderful book on the relevant period and it was very readable. It was understandable. It was easily assimilated—and did not a question come up in our exam which lay exactly along the lines of one of its chapters. Most of us, I reckon, used this chapter and read the sardonic note on returned scripts, 'This is very good but Sayles did it rather better!' We were marked down. Our dependent thought had been recognised and we were penalised accordingly.

The point I am trying to get through to you is that we are trained to be of independent mind from early stages. Burns spoke highly of the man of independent mind and of course there is a sense in which this is good. We should not blow about with every wind that passes. To have no mind of our own can be dangerous and in one sense it is desirable to have an independent mind, but independent from what? Independent from the minds of others—yes, but when we are dealing with God it is not a good thing since we ought to be dependent upon God. This background training in independence can suddenly become a weakness because there is in us a part that will hold ourselves independent of God as well as of others. That is a rock on which many perish.

So Satan comes along and says first, 'You've got a very good mind,' and most people are susceptible to flattery. 'You've certainly got a much better mind than X, Y and Z,' and you concur. 'It is good,' says he, 'to be independent. Don't give way. Think things out for yourself—be logical and understand where you are going.' Now, what people don't realise is that by doing this they raise an altar to the human mind and they enthrone reason as though by human thought and human reason you can reach ultimate truth and reality. This is to enthrone the mind and I want you to listen to this very, very carefully because it is of fundamental importance. Reason was given to man by God and reason does, ideally, reflect an ultimate reality. Reason should not be abandoned. It should not be discarded but it should be viewed in the light of the Fall. We need to reach back in our thinking to the place where reason was at the beginning— not to reason affected by the Fall but to reason in its first perfection.

My insight into this has largely come from observing what happens when an individual is functioning under the power of the Holy Spirit. In that hour there is a denial of self. There is a denial of the power of the mind to initiate any kind of action and there is an openness to God. Suddenly the mind is flooded by God. There comes Divine illumination and thought processes are quickened. The person concerned does not initiate thought but receives thought. He transmits thought that is not his own but which comes from another source. I believe that this helps us to understand what happened in the beginning. When our first father was made a thinking creature he was given a

28

mind that would receive the thought of the Divine Mind.
His mind was to be like a radio receiver. He was not to
function on his own and transmit on his own but to be
rooted in God, grounded in God. He was to receive from
God and transmit what God gave. In the hour man took his
own way and broke the connection with God, he still had a
mind and he still had reasoning powers, but he swung free
from his base and did his own thinking. He did his own
imagining. He decided his own actions where formerly he
had not thought for himself but received thought as God led
him. Now he was out of touch with the Divine. With
redemption and the Baptism in the Spirit, the mind begins
to come back under Divine control in a measure and the
position changes. Instead of thinking our own foolish
thoughts we come into a position where we can say, 'I don't
know but I can find out as God reveals.'

I found the outworking of this principle last night. I
could not in a thousand years have found by myself the
theme that God wants to take for this week at Camp. I could
have had many wonderful ideas. It is not difficult to have
ideas—but I couldn't provide ideas that would live, that
would sparkle, that would shine, that would have the
anointing of God upon them. I was totally dependent on the
action of the Divine. I was totally dependent and am still
dependent upon the revelation of God. Suddenly a person
can be free of mental bondage and acknowledge the need for
God. There can come a flash from God and the sense of the
touch of God. Such a vessel suddenly realises that he is
coming into and indeed is in the kind of place for which he
has been redeemed. He is under Divine control.

Satan wants to grip the thinking processes and if he can
do this he holds a fearful control. There are many of you
who have found great difficulty in having your minds totally
cleared. Sometimes in taking a series on 'death to self' I deal
with the mind and it becomes evident that it is a most

29

difficult area to have set free. More difficult I think than the will, more difficult even than the heart. The mind is of exceeding difficulty. You will try to assert your right to think to the very last ditch.

You may be about to preach. You may be going to minister in exorcism or some other spiritual realm and Satan will try to intervene and get you to think about other things. Of course, you instinctively know that in such an hour you are not there to think your own thoughts but to reflect God. You are to give the word of God. You are not there to argue or become involved at any kind of human reasoning level with a demon or anybody else. You are there to declare the word of the living God and to emanate the life of God. You are something other than a mere thinking person. Satan brings his batteries strongly to affect and control thought and there may come a fear on you, 'But I can't afford to stop thinking. I can't afford to cut that line and not be dependent on my own thought.' In other words, 'I cannot afford to trust God!' This is what it boils down to.

Now let me assure you that when you go out on the road that I am indicating you don't stop being a thinking creature. You become far more a thinking creature than you have ever been in all your life. Your mind becomes flooded with thought—creative, wonderful, glorious, logical, flawless, Divine. You do not become a zombie. You do not become an automaton but you do begin to function at the highest levels in the sphere for which you were born. You are a receiver of thought rather than an initiator of it.

So Satan says, 'You have a good mind and it is right to be a man, a woman, of independent thought. Keep a grip on your thinking. Never let that go.' I reply, 'Well now, you've got a good mind, have you? How good? What do you mean by good?' 'Well, better than a lot of people.' Supposing it was the best mind in town, I want you to observe the worth of good minds, the good minds of all the world combined.

By being good the minds of men have all reached the same conclusions, haven't they? All men are living admirably at peace with one another. They all see things the same way, because having good minds they all think alike. Well, maybe not really—the Russians and the Americans don't just see everything totally eye to eye. But we'll not bother about that lot. Many of them are not Christians so it maybe doesn't apply to them, but with the Christians that's a different matter. Then take all the Christians of all the ages past and present. They had and have good minds so they all thought and think alike? Well, no, the Brethren and the Pentecostal folk don't always agree, and the Baptists have got some notions of their own and so have the Anglicans, and the Roman Catholics are out on a different line. So the good minds all seem to be reaching different conclusions. Maybe the human mind is not all that it's cracked up to be. And God would bring the pressure more keenly and He would press you to the point: 'Do human minds, on the ground of cold logic, inevitably reach the same conclusions?' The whole of history seems to disprove it. 'But I am going to trust my own mind.' My friend, millions have done it and they've reached millions of different conclusions. Do you think that *you* are going to hit the jackpot, that *you* are going to arrive at ultimate truth because your mind is better than all of theirs? Have you ever realised the diversity of human thought, the diversity even of the thoughts of the professors of theology across the universities of the world—the profound differences?—and probably many of them in their pride had thought, 'I've got it. I've found it. I've found the road. I've thought it through.'

One of the things that research scholars find in reaching what they hope is ultimate truth or the last word on a matter is that in a few years (if they are lucky—a few weeks if they are less lucky) somebody else is going to publish something that puts their conclusions quite out of court.

I have a daughter who has a book on Chinese philosophy about to be published but she'll be fortunate if somebody else isn't ahead of her by the time the book gets into print. Life's like that. You think you've got the last word and somebody else has a word after it and a few years later somebody else shows how foolish you were in this idea and that idea and the other idea and yet people say, 'I'll think it out. I'll think it out. I'll establish truth.'

It reminds me of a school staff who were going to win the pools. Nearly all groups who start to support Littlewoods are going to win the pools, no question about it, and I asked the Maths. Principal what the chances were. It was a very awkward question, apart from the mathematical calculation. The chances were millions to one against—millions to one against winning the pools—and the idea that you will think yourself through by the power of your own mind to ultimate truth is many millions to one against. Your mind wasn't built for that. It wasn't fitted for that. It's like trying to cross the Atlantic on a bicycle. Bicycles weren't built for that and neither was your mind built for finding God and ultimate truth. If you listen to wisdom you'll begin to see it. Even from the point of view of logic it's illogical. By applying human thought itself to the problem you can see the fallacy of the enthronement of the mind. Its destruction, or the seeds of its destruction, lie within itself. You cannot do it that way. And God comes closer and He says, 'What has been the result of your thought processes and your imaginations?' And you say, 'Well, to be quite truthful I haven't got very far on the road of righteousness but in my imaginations I've got quite a way down the road of wickedness and sin. Lord, if I'm being honest I've got to acknowledge that I haven't only got a weak mind in the sense of reaching ultimates, but I've got a polluted mind in the sense of feeding on the unclean. Lord, I am beginning to see—I need a new mind. I need to be on a new basis altogether. I

32

am going to tear down the altar to human reason which feeds human pride and I'm going to come very low and I'm going to say, O God, be merciful to me, a sinner. Give me a new mind, give me a mind that is patterned after the mind of the Lord Jesus. I want a renewed mind. I want You, Lord, to breathe upon my thinking processes and change me and cause me to be aware when I am going off on my own and stop me. I want to become sensitive to Your whisper and listen for it and respond to it until Christ in me begins to think His thoughts through me: until He begins to transmit through me: until I have a mind that is garrisoned, that is holding out all wrong thinking and wrong notions, a mind that is tuned to receive the Divine.' And you know, God will begin to do that very thing and you will walk with revelation and it may be that you will be used in the giving of prophetic utterance because you have the mind of God. 'Let this mind be in you which was also in Christ Jesus.' The crucifixion is perhaps most difficult for those of us who are most independent. The crucifixion for people who are used to handling their own affairs and making their own decisions can be very difficult indeed but when you come on a life that has found the secret of having yielded the bastion of the mind, you come on a saint, on one who is almost certain to be very deeply used of God.

I have started at the head. It is the last bastion and the most difficult of all to yield, and God brings His mighty forces to win that fort and Satan moves his heavy troops to defend the strong point and to keep a grip.

When you begin to understand the realm of exorcism and demon possession you will learn that demons affect various parts of the body but they tend ultimately to go for vital centres. Again and again they go for the mind and try to bring the thinking processes under their control, and woe to the one whose mind is gripped by those wicked ones. He or she is no longer a person of independent thought but one who is affected and perhaps later dominated by demonic thought until there is a terror of disobeying the voice of darkness. The enemy wants to possess the human mind totally and so does God and you are in the middle. This is the first strong point that we are taking in this series—the first fort. With whom are you going to side? Forget yourself because you are like a chattel. You are like a pawn in the game. The two main forces are doing battle for control of the mind of man. As for me, I want to have the mind of God. If you have the mind of Satan and things go to their ultimate you will get to a stage where you are driven and can do nothing about it. Driven of evil—your mind possessed of evil—driven like a straw in the wind.

Occasionally we are shocked by some horrendous crime. We read our daily paper and we find that somebody has been guilty of a foul kind of murder that we just can't understand. As the person is quoted we have a feeling he doesn't understand either. Occasionally he will say, 'I was driven to it. I couldn't help myself. I felt something inside me telling me to do it.' If you become more familiar with this side of life you may come to the conclusion, 'Yes, friend, that's true. You were driven to it. You so allowed yourself to be possessed of an evil power and your mind was so gripped that you became like a straw in the wind under the blowing power of hell.'

'Oh,' you say, 'I thought I thought for myself.' Did you? Did you? I often speak from the position of an older person, comparatively speaking, to a lot of quite young folk and I feel I have fought the same battle through the years with generation after generation. The battleground doesn't really change a great deal. It remains fairly static and I find generation after generation full of the pride of human intellect and by action despising the leading of the Divine.

I remember my University days. I had been baptised in the Spirit and realised the glory of Divine revelation. I had come from a religious background where the mind was greatly exalted and I remember the emphasis on 'getting down to the meat of the Word'. What was really intended was to get down to a merely intellectual interpretation of the Bible. There was a deal of pride in the attitude. This was not the highway to spirituality. God wants us to have a knowledge of the Word, but He wants much more than that. He wants the Word to be alive within us.

I remember being in the Hebrides in the aftermath of revival when folks from the south were questioning, 'Do these new converts know, for example, who wrote the Book of Galatians and would they know its historical background?' These Highland people were not worried one little bit about who wrote the Book of Galatians—the Book of Galatians fed their spirits. They ate and drank the Book of Galatians and other books as well. Some of them were as spiritual princes compared to the person who was worried about this kind of detail. Being born in revival they were, as they say in the Highlands, 'well-born'. Their spirits were sensitive to God. Some of them were nearer God in a few hours after conversion than many are after years of profession. As though studying the Bible as an intellectual exercise is itself a first priority! Now I am not wanting in any way to pour cold water on a genuine understanding of the Word. I have sought this myself through all my years, but to exalt the intellectual side of it to the place that some do is greatly mistaken. There is a type of head knowledge that 'puffs up', to use Bible language. The knowledge of God, on the other hand, is of vital importance and tends to humility. Let the knowledge He gives come in its place and in its time. There is a place for the illumination of the mind, make no mistake about that. I am not in any way speaking against the true knowledge of the Word, but beware of the idea that you are growing up spiritually simply because you understand a little more of the Bible intellectually. You may, in fact, be retrogressing. Let the Word feed you. Let it change you into the image of Christ. Get your priorities right. Become men and women of God to whom and through whom the Word comes—a Word that may never have been spoken before—the Word relevant to a circumstance and an occasion, given by the Divine.

So, in conclusion—whose side are you on? Who is going to win the citadel of your mind—God or Satan?

Note

[1] These studies, including an additional chapter 'The Power and the Glory,' are published in *Consider Him* (New Dawn Books, 1988).

3

The Eye and the Ear

Satan looks for those parts in our personality where there are weaknesses and he brings tremendous force to bear that he might crush us, break us, devour us, destroy us; and God is also interested in our weak areas that He might strengthen us. He wants us to be able not only to resist Satan but to become so strong that we can attack his kingdom.

That is the kind of general picture I want you to have in your mind. In the first of our studies the part that was under dispute by the two commanders was the mind and you will find that I will be dealing with parts of the body from the head downwards. I started with the mind and this is an area in which there is tremendous conflict between good and evil.

We now move from the mind to the eyes and the ears. I will take the eyes first. Now Satan is very interested in eye-gate, very interested indeed. He wants to fill your vision and Satan being Satan wants to fill it with things filthy, with things sordid, with things degrading, with material things, with worldly things. Oh, he has a tremendous variety of things with which to fill the human vision and this is an extremely vulnerable part of the human make-up. Indeed there are three parts that are particularly dangerous—so much so that Christ took them specifically. He said: 'If thine EYE offend thee, pluck it out, and cast it from thee; it is better for thee to enter into life with one eye, rather than having two eyes to be cast into hell fire,' where the worm dieth not and the flame is not quenched. The second was the hand and the third the foot. The eye—the thing that you see. The hand—the thing that you do. The foot—the place that you go. Rather than be a castaway soul cut them off. It is as though the battle can become so intense that rather than be overwhelmed you should cut your losses. You are better to cut these things off than be totally overwhelmed—but a good commander defends the post. God wants these things for Himself.

We'll just perhaps look a little more closely before rushing on in the tempest of battle. Eye-gate. The young generation probably has little idea of what life was like thirty, forty, fifty years ago, when it was comparatively clean—really comparatively clean. You could pick up most daily newspapers and be unashamed. There are many of them now that you wouldn't be seen reading in any public place. Indeed, I had an exceedingly embarrassing experience the day before I came to Camp. I was minded to go into the country and see a brother who has had a slight shock. He's about ten years older than myself. One of my sisters lost her husband about a fortnight ago and as it happened she was going to be in a house within a hundred yards of my brother. I thought, 'I'll take them some ice cream.' When I was a boy in the country, ice cream was a great treat and I know a shop which has wonderful ice cream so I got two square tubs. I had learned earlier that if you want to keep ice cream over a long period you should wrap it in newspaper. This gives very good insulation and so the shopkeeper got out a paper and halved it, wrapping the first and then the second tub. I looked at one of them, and I *never*, but *never*, in all my life saw such degrading filth as I saw in that paper. I think there were literally about twenty pictures of half-naked bodies. It was polluted. It was grim. It was just so bad that I couldn't possibly be associated with it even remotely. Now, most of you probably know television better than I do because I don't have one, but I have been in houses from time to time when suddenly to the embarrassment of the householders the programmes have suddenly switched and without warning become extremely filthy. I know too from school experience that some of the videos that are advertised and are available are highly objectionable.

I remember from boyhood in a comparatively clean age that you needed to see only one or two vaguely suggestive things (there wasn't much of it but there was a little occasionally) for these pictures to go into the mind and to take a grip of the mind and be remembered. You needed to hear only a few filthy little poems of two, three or four lines for them to have a lasting impact—and these were very, very clean days compared to the days in which we now live. This is a day in which there are sewers emptying their filth into our living-rooms, right into our houses—cesspools of iniquity, devil sludge—and there are so many who are lapping it up.

'That is a horrible thing to say.' It's not half as horrible as what people are doing. The filth goes in and pollutes and poisons and nobody needs to come and tell me that I am exaggerating, laying it on too thick. I am at the other end, friend. I am there when these filthy demons which are behind it come screaming out of human bodies, screaming their filth into my ear as they come out. Does that shock you? I am there when it happens. I am angry when I think of it—of what I have witnessed as I have seen men and women delivered under the hand of God, delivered from the filth of a sexually perverted age. Oh, I have known a person in the very midst of it shout that they were going deeper in because as they were remembering the occasions of pollution they were going down and down. I have had to stand aside until Christ himself in that case came and took the matter into His own hands. It is an age of extreme filth and it is far worse than most of you have any idea of. Let me tell you this—there are very few young people who come to Christ these days who don't require exorcism. They are polluted at such an early stage and it gets worse and worse. If it is not sorted it deepens and it doesn't go away automatically. So it is with sexual perversion and uncleanness and lust. These don't go away because you look elsewhere. They go down deep and grip.

I could keep you here all day telling you stories. There is one that comes back to me almost like a nightmare. A man turned to Christ, I believe genuinely, in so far as he could. He ultimately realised his need for deliverance and he came at a time when Miss Taylor[1] was moving very powerfully in this realm with visual ministry also in operation, and she described this man's condition. She said that he was in a terrible state. It was almost as though there were demons dripping from every pore of his body. In the hour he came for ministry he was absolutely petrified. The demons were talking to him and telling him he would die if he went on with this. They would kill him. Danger! Run for your life! And that great strong man was absolutely terrified. He got on to his feet and burst out that door, right out of the church and we never saw him again. Absolutely terrified, the demons were, of the power of God.

I told you yesterday about the battle for the mind. The demons seek to take control until the mind is driven. They have the power to drive if we give way to them. We are in battle in this our day and generation. Things are worse than most of us imagine; the lid has come off and the foam of hell is spattered around.

If, on that wall there, the Lord Jesus wrote what I think

He wrote on the ground when the woman was taken in adultery and her accusers were about to stone her, how would you fare? He said, 'Let him that is without sin cast the first stone...' and stooping down He wrote on the ground. We are never told what He wrote but I think we can infer it because starting from the oldest to the youngest they began to go out. Just imagine that against our every name there was written our every sinful thought, every sinful word, every sinful action. In due time it would come down to your name and I am dealing at the moment specifically with impurity. Just imagine it all written there—every impure thought, every lust, every deed, every visual image of which you would be ashamed. I tell you, one by one from the oldest to the youngest we would go out. Could you stand seeing it all written there? Although the Church has been invaded by the codes of the world, God doesn't change and His law doesn't change. Where do you stand this morning in relation to Christ's standard of purity? The Law said, 'Thou shalt not commit adultery'; He said, 'He that looketh on a woman to lust after her hath committed adultery with her already in his heart.' Christ demands truth in the inward parts right to the bottom of the being. He demands purity.

There's great joy in purity. There's great power in it. A person suddenly discovers there's something positive in it. There's something wonderful in it. It's not just, 'Don't, don't, don't, don't!' It's, 'Do, do, do, do!' When you get purity you get power. You get freedom. You get liberty. You get a glorious two-handed sword in your hands and you go out and ruin the kingdom of Satan. It's one of the most wonderful joys I think you will ever have in time. I don't know about eternity but certainly one of the greatest joys I ever know on earth is when the mighty power of the Holy Spirit is upon me and there is a sword in my hand. It's wonderful, and the heel of Christ is on the head of the serpent and he's shouting in his agony. It's glorious, and I find as that wonderful power comes on me I can shout, 'Hallelujah!' with the best of them. I can tell you it's, 'Praise the Lord!' all right as the serpent squirms and the demons flee His presence. Oh yes, it's related to purity—purity in the inner heart, in the inner thought, in the inner spirit. Purity and power are linked together. I don't fully understand wherein the great joy comes but I do know this—that if that mighty afflatus of the Holy Spirit comes on me, and God is glorified and Satan is routed, I can tingle long after it with joy, with the surging joy of the Holy Ghost. Wonderful, glorious life indeed!

So Satan's forces come up against eye-gate and you say, 'Well, to be quite honest, I like Satan's provision. It appeals to me. I do quite like to get a hold of that dirty magazine when nobody knows anything about it. It gives me quite a pleasure to flick through it.' Do you know that sometimes a comparatively clean-minded person gets a magazine like that and flicks through it once in a lifetime and is soiled, and sometimes it's years later before he is set free from the consequence of it?

You say, 'Oh, I didn't think it would have been as bad as that.' If I tell you anthrax is absolutely deadly you don't go fooling around with it. An animal gets it. You burn the animal—absolutely burn it. There's no question, no fooling around, no cutting off a bit hoping you can eat it. The lot is burned. It is treated seriously. 'Oh no, it will be all right for me to read the magazine. I am a man of independent mind. I can keep it out.' So flick, flick, flick, flick—visual memories that rise in the night-time, rise through the weeks and the months and soil the soul and give entry to evil entities. That is how it works.

People sometimes say to me, 'How do demons get in?' I'll tell you how demons get in all right—on a whole lot of fronts. I know how demons get in. I have almost literally seen them coming in as well as going out. I have no difficulty in telling you how demons get in—most people have them in because they are fools and they open doors and they whistle them in by their actions. Not very nice, is it?[2]

It reminds me of medical students. I presume it's not very nice to cut up cadavers. For ordinary human beings like you and me it is something to be avoided but for the students it seems to be the spice of life almost, and it may be that this kind of spiritual dissection is not to everyone's taste, but sometimes you've got to face nasty things as well as pleasant things and what the devil is feeding through eye-gate is something nasty, filthy, the scum of hell, the kind of thing which those of you who go out of life lost souls will have for ever. You'll have lust that is never satisfied but which goes on endlessly seeking and never finding fulfilment. The broth of hell has spilled over on to earth and men and women are affected and polluted by the foulness of it. Satan attacks eye-gate. 'Bring the forces against eye-gate. There are very few who aren't so proud that they think they can look without danger at my pictures, and I'll provide them. I have my minions who, for money, will provide them. Yes, into the national papers on to page three. I'll provide the pictures. I'll flood the television. I'll flood the videos. I'll bring my forces against eye-gate and they are already disposed to look my way, in their curiosity, and in their pride and in their lust.'

And what says God? God is a conqueror. God is no defeatist Commander and God brings up His forces to deal with eye-gate. And He teaches you that in the moment you go that way you become less of a person. You become a shadow of what you could be. You become weak. Instead of having the clean, clear eye that can look any man or woman in the face there comes a dark scance and a shadow and a drooping of the eyes because the dirt can be seen. Always remember that, friends. The dirt in your spirit can be seen by some of us who have that ability. I can look across a congregation and again and again I can pick them out. I can pick out people who are in sexual trouble. It is written as clearly in their faces as though the mark of Cain was on the forehead. It reflects in the eyes and it reflects almost in a scance of the skin. Did you know that?

If you have any real character you just can't stand being in that kind of bondage, and God in His great love teaches people step by step. He shows them that they can't have it both ways and He strengthens men and women in their resolve. He sets gifts in the church whereby a man can be set free from the bondages and tyrannies of Satan on these fronts. He feeds them with Christ until the purity of Christ becomes attractive and Christ begins to dwell in them and they begin to take control. They take a grip of themselves and they receive power over the enemy in their own lives and in the lives of others, and holiness becomes increasingly attractive.

He shows you what kind of things you ought to think about, the kind of things you ought to look at, things that are pure and clean and holy and of good report. You fill your vision with that which is good instead of that which is filthy. You change the one for the other and you look Christward. Let me say again that both God and Satan are interested in the same vital parts of the body—first the mind and now the eyes. To God eye-gate is very important, so important that you'd be better to have no eyes at all than to go to hell as a result of what you see. Better to be blind than to be polluted. It's as strong as that in the counsels of God. After looking at the position from both sides I want you to stand aside for a moment and look at Christ. Look at the eyes of Christ.

Did it ever occur to you that as you grow into the maturity of a child of God you too will have eyes like the eyes of Christ—compassionate, loving, stern, unbearable in holiness? Do you realise it is given to the sons of man to be so taken over by Christ that the demons will scream out too, unable to stand the divine presence in you and me? Not just God somewhere far away, but Christ who walked the shores of earth walking again in you and me—men and women of God so deeply in God now that the demonic powers are disturbed.

I ask you this morning, friend. Do you prefer to be under the bondage of Satan in corruption, rolling, wallowing in it, or do you want to be a man or a woman set free into the wonderful freedom and liberty of the sons of God—an overcomer, a destroyer of that evil, wicked, foul sex-perverted kingdom? Which way? Have you the courage to rise and say no to your fallen nature that the nature of the risen Christ might be in you? Sometimes I note that people don't get free until they confess their degradation. When that stage is reached, frequently the binding power is broken. Never fool with uncleanness in any sense of that word. It has a bitter bite back.

We'll leave eye-gate now and come to the next bastion that is of interest to the rival commanders—ear-gate. Wherein is Satan's interest in ear-gate? That's the very place into which he pours his suggestions—where else? You listen to his voice. You say, 'Oh, I don't remember Satan ever speaking to me.' Well, some of you do know that Satan has spoken to you, but many of you have probably heard his voice frequently and not been aware of his identity. It may be that he has normally come to you as an angel of light and you heard the voice but you didn't recognise the source. But let's come to even simpler, more natural things. You've heard the voice of your fellow men. You've heard the voices of other Christians. Has it ever occurred to you how much poison has poured into your heart and spirit through the things that you have listened to—the things that you have heard, subtle suggestions? 'You know so and so...yes? Did you hear about...(some little juicy bits of scandal)?' 'No, do you tell me?' 'Oh yes, it's true. Don't tell anybody. You wouldn't want that sort of thing to be spread around. It's not nice, you know. It would hurt them and it would do them harm.' 'Oh, no, it's all right—you can trust me... Did you hear? Don't tell anybody. I got it in confidence,' and lo, it goes round and round like that.

I remember being extremely disgusted a long time ago. There had been a local scandal and a retired policeman I happened to know vaguely was absolutely wallowing in it. Into everybody's ear he could find he was pouring details of this terrible scandal and talking as though he was quite shocked and he was nothing of the kind shocked, nothing of the kind. I hear people sometimes refer to a bit of scandal, 'You know, I can't believe it. I just can't believe it,' and I say, 'There goes a right hypocrite. I can believe it quite easily. I know the part in me that could do this, that and the other.' I know the human heart and people who hold up their hands in horror at normal sinfulness are nearly always hypocrites. Oh they may be surprised indeed that a particular person did that. It's when they go a bit further as though they are shocked at human nature being able to do such and such that I question their honesty.

Now I know there are extremes. There are the muggings and raping of old women, for example, that are almost impossible to understand. I am not talking about that. Ordinary people do find that difficult to understand but the normal stuff of scandal, people understand perfectly well.

So, into your ear comes the scandal. That's actually not always so alarming. Into your ear comes the criticism and Satan is particularly keen to have the emissaries of Christ criticised: the people whom God is using torn down[3]. 'Try to level them. Try to make them like ourselves. Try to discover their human weaknesses. Try to take away their authority. Try to kill God's appointed leaders.' Through ear-gate the shafts come. You listen and your spirit is weakened. Through ear-gate television has its appeal.

Through ear-gate comes the pop music. 'Well, we're a young crowd. Things change from generation to generation. Things differ you know. Your generation, oh it was classical music then and that leaves us cold. We want something with a kick.' So you get something with a kick—sometimes brewed in hell under deep black magic influences, with horrible words and music combined. Ah yes, some of the converted Africans can tell you. I understand that recently some of them expressed wonder that we allow demons to come into our churches through music. 'What do you mean?' Don't you know? Don't you realise that that particular beat is how they come in? There's music which, per se, without a word to it, is demonic—just recognise that. Its influence is dark and polluted. 'Oh no, no. It's just music.' It's not just music. Music is an extremely strong conductor of good or of evil and it can be in the beat and in the tempo.

Now I am no expert in this. I can't particularly distinguish except perhaps at the extremes. I could probably be easily deceived. I am very unmoved by a great deal of music. I could listen to a pop programme. I'd be bored out of my mind almost but I wouldn't be corrupted. To me it would be painful and tedious but not dangerous. But there are others and with them the beat goes in, the beat goes in and you can see it, and you can feel it in their movements and reactions. Sometimes when they come to me for help they'll say, 'You know, I can't get it out of my being. I can't get rid of it. I can't get free of it. It's there. It's there. It goes on and on.' They may need exorcism. Sometimes it is the greatest pull back into the world that they have to fight with. Now I don't understand all of what I'm telling you. I know about it but I don't understand it in the sense of empathising with it. I have never been in any danger from it. It has no appeal for me. I don't empathise. I don't enter in but I've got to deal with the effects of it in others. Take my word for it, there's much of it that is associated with the black arts and sometimes fairly openly so. There's a deliberate move of Satan to catch an emotional part of mankind through this ear filth. There is eye filth and there is ear filth and Satan says, 'Bring up the forces, bring up the forces and let's take ear-gate too and hold it. Pour our reserves through it. Let the streams of corruption flow that way.' And God says, 'No, I want your ear. I want your ear. I want you to shut your ear to every voice that is not My voice, to the voice of Satan, to the voice of his minions, to the voice of men with their varied opinions which are not of Me. I want you to shut your ear to the voice of your closest friends in Christ when these voices in any way conflict with My voice.'

Oh, let me get this through to you. Those of you who as yet don't know us well will need to know this sooner or later. We don't believe in a personality cult of any kind in this Movement. Leaders don't assume a position where they lord it over others. We don't build a position where there are little dictators. We don't ask or expect people to lean on us. I do know that at the beginning a new-born soul needs to have support. I don't mean that they should never lean, but as quickly as possible it is our policy to have an individual leaning on Christ, feeding directly from Christ, in touch with Christ—not merely hearing our voices but hearing the voice of God, not having an ear open so much to us as hearing the voice of God Himself—to be in a position that if I, for example, was giving wrong advice they would still be in a position to hear the voice of God. No man is infallible and it's a very wrong thing for us ever to try to assume a position that only the Holy One Himself should occupy. Our job is to have souls dependent on the Living God.

You will find, however, that as you become more and more God-dependent you will become closer and closer to those who are walking with God and hearing His voice, and sometimes you will need others with you in dark and difficult hours. God has so arranged it. There should be unity within the church and its leadership—a unity in humility of spirit, a walking with God, but a growing up in Christ, a deepening in Christ Himself—a knowledge of Christ.

In talking to my daughter, Mary, I have noticed that very seldom do I ask for her opinion nor does she ask for mine. I am, however, supremely interested when she tells me that God has spoken to her. What I am interested in is what God has revealed to her. She could come to me and say, 'What do you think about the next Camp? I think such and such.' I may be interested in a vague, general way. My manners are good enough for me to listen but that's about all. But when she comes speaking in a different way altogether and says, 'I believe that God is showing me that it will be thus and thus,' I give that full attention.

This cuts very deeply actually. Something else suddenly strikes me. There are times when some of you who are back-sliding, playing the fool, come and say what you are proposing to do and how far you are going and this and that. Occasionally a person gets an awful shock when I say, 'I am not interested in what you think you are going to do. I am only interested in God's side of this matter. I am interested in what God will allow you to do. Do you realise that He may not allow you to come back? The first concern is not whether you think of coming back or whether you will want to come back. That may be of little significance. What is significant is whether the possibility will still exist for you to retrace the steps. I am not particularly interested in what *you* think. I am vitally interested in the *Divine* side of it.' That cuts a person down to proper size and it happens also to be the truth. People are so bombastic and bumptious. 'Oh, I think I will do this. I will do that. I will do the other and won't it be wonderful. I will make my return. Put out a red carpet.' Well, we haven't got a stock of red carpets. 'But am I not important?' No, indeed you are not (although in another sense you are so important that Christ died for you). 'Does it not matter desperately to all the world what I do?' No! You know what God said to Oswald Chambers? 'Young man, I want you in My service but I can do without you,' and He left him at that. This was in an hour of crisis—a moment of decision. 'I want you in My service but I can do without you.' That cut him right down to size and by God's grace Oswald Chambers took God's way and was mightily used. You see, if you take the wrong way you are not important at all. C. S. Lewis puts it wonderfully well in *The Great Divorce*. There a poor soul who had refused God's way became less and less of a substantial being and ultimately dropped through a crack in Heaven's floor. That is all the significance you have if you go the wrong way but if you go God's way you will be mightily important, not as a person in your own right but as a container of God. Only in His hand will you ever be of the slightest importance; otherwise you are a non-event. I mean that. I am as serious as a judge. Let me say it again: I mean that—otherwise you are a non-event. Oh, people sometimes depart in the pride and vanity of their hearts as though something inportant had gone away. It reminds me of what God said about Pharaoh if I may paraphrase, 'You are but a noise, only a noise.' Let's get a true sight of ourselves and our relative importance.

The trouble is that many of us were spoiled as children. Mummy thought you were wonderful and you grew up thinking you were wonderful. Fifty years ago the maxim was that children should be seen and not heard. You had it drilled into you that you were a nobody and of very little importance. One of your highest functions for many a day was to run messages for your elders and to keep quiet. A very different world was the world of fifty years ago. The scene has changed and one result can be seen in the arrogance and pride on the faces of many young people. 'It is important what I do. I am significant. Oh, I am important.' Well, as a leader, it is my responsibility to rid you of this idea to the best of my ability. You are not and in so far as you do not put on the nature of Christ you are a nobody and a nothing and of no significance. But in so far as you put on Christ Jesus you become a somebody. He shines through you and you become a glory. You become worth having been created. You don't fall through a hole or a crack in Heaven's floor but you ascend into eternal glory, a son of the Living God, a daughter of a King—grown and developed. And Satan gathers his harvest—a multitude of nonentities—and you go duped into the darkness or you go, by way of crucifixion of all the old carnal nature, into the glory of God.

Now which commander are you going to put in charge of ear-gate? Is it the Living God and are you prepared to keep out everything that does not come through Him? The same with eye-gate. Will you allow Him to stand sentinel at these gates and sift everything and feed you with His own glorious sights and sounds—the sight of glory, the vision of God, the sounds of Heaven, the sounds of Heavenly music, song in the spirit, the glory of the words of God, a vision splendid, a voice like the sound of many waters—the voice of God?

Finally—the ears of Christ. He heard no evil. He thought no evil. He imagined no evil. His ear was tuned to the Heavenly Father. There in the wilderness when Satan tried to whisper in His ear He renounced the voice. He said (if I may paraphrase), 'That's not My Father's voice.' He remembered the word of God and He quoted it to Satan again and again. He gave no place whatever to the words of Satan. His ears were holy ears. You see, we've got to have all controlled by God. You'll find the truth of this as we go down the body—the mind divinely illumined and garrisoned, the eyes divinely guarded and controlled, the ears shut and open at His command.

Shall we go God's road?

Notes

[1] See this lady's testimony in the author's *A Trumpet Call to Women* (New Dawn Books, 1988).

[2] For fuller information on this whole subject, readers are referred to 'Discernment—and Exorcism' in the author's *Reflections on the Gifts of the Spirit* (New Dawn Books, 1988).

[3] There are cases, of course, where sin is open and criticism unavoidable.

4

The Tongue and the Shoulders

Most of you know the line that the morning studies have been taking and I believe there has been some conjecture amongst you as to which part of the body will come next. Some have facetiously suggested the nose! Well, it has its purposes—but it is not, in fact, the part that comes next on the list. I have come down a little way to the tongue and I imagine you will find it difficult to forecast what the subjects for the rest of the week will be—but do try.

I want to read from the Epistle of James. I don't know whether you've ever noticed that James is very explicit in what he has to say. Shall we read from chapter 3, from part way through verse 2:

> If any stumbleth not in word, the same is a perfect man, able to bridle the whole body also. Now if we put the horses' bridles into their mouths, that they may obey us, we turn about their whole body also. Behold, the ships also, though they are so great, and are driven by rough winds, are yet turned about by a very small rudder, whither the impulse of the steersman willeth. So the tongue also is a little member, and boasteth great things. Behold, how much wood is kindled by how small a fire! And the tongue is a fire: the world of iniquity among our members is the

tongue, which defileth the whole body and setteth on fire the wheel of nature, and is set on fire by hell. For every kind of beasts and birds, of creeping things and things in the sea, is tamed, and hath been tamed by mankind: but the tongue can no man tame; it is a restless evil, it is full of deadly poison. Therewith bless we the Lord and Father; and therewith curse we men, which are made after the likeness of God: out of the same mouth cometh forth blessing and cursing. My brethren, these things ought not so to be. Doth the fountain send forth from the same opening sweet water and bitter? Can a fig tree, my brethren, yield olives, or a vine figs? Neither can salt water yield sweet (James 3:2–12).

I think it will not be difficult for you to appreciate this morning that both Satan and God are interested in the tongue. First let me say that Satan looks on the tongue as a peculiarly useful part to have under his control and influence.

It is easy to understand that if a person is given to bad language and filthy talk Satan is likely to have a grip on him. Many of us are apt to acknowledge this and dismiss the matter at that point but this, in fact, is not the end of the matter at all. The tongue is extremely potent and there are many other ways in which it is abused.

As I pondered on this theme my mind went back a little way in history and I recollected some of the uses of language. Those of you who have studied Shakespeare may remember the famous speech of Antony after the murder of Caesar. He turns the crowd against Brutus in a most skilful way. He swings a whole multitude by the use of words. We come up nearer our own day. Pitt the Elder had a tremendous command of language and could hold Parliament spellbound and get a great deal of his own way. So it was with Gladstone and in very recent times with Churchill. Many of you will know of some of his famous speeches and the effect that these had on a whole nation. I remember listening to his speech when Britain had been reduced to a very sad state and was threatened with seemingly imminent invasion. I can recall that gravelly voice, an accent that is very difficult to imitate (it resulted from a physical defect):

> We shall not flag or fail. We shall fight in France, we shall fight on the seas and oceans, we shall fight with growing confidence and growing strength in the air, we shall defend our island, whatever the cost may be, we shall fight on the beaches, we shall fight in the fields and in the streets, we shall fight in the hills; we shall never surrender.[1]

and as he is supposed to have commented, covering the microphone,

> and we'll hit them over the head with beer bottles for it's all that we've got left!

The nation was stirred and deeply moved by the part they did hear. Fortunately they did not hear the other bit. Whether it is true or apocryphal I have never been absolutely sure—but he had quite a sense of humour had Churchill. The power of language—it stirred and thrilled a nation. It strengthened the backbone. It stirred to war. He dealt with the French generals' prediction that Britain would have her neck wrung like a chicken: 'Some chicken—some neck!' to the amusement of the nation. Then there came the memorable words about the Battle of Britain pilots, 'Never in the field of human conflict was so much owed by so many to so few,' and they in their pawky way suggested he was referring to the mess bills!

Then there was Hitler. I can't speak German but here is my imitation. [Readers are left to use their imaginations here.] You could feel something running and rippling through people as he addressed them and sent them out to tragedy—all through the power of language, the power of the tongue.

In a strange way the tongue can be a vehicle for the devil

himself, and through it he can hypnotise men. That brings us to an interesting consideration. That part in a person which can be hypnotised or which can come under hypnotic influence is itself God-given and this is something many people forget. There is a proper function for this part of the human personality. It is not given to come under the control of an evil entity or of another human but it is designed to come under the control of the Holy Spirit and when the power of the Holy Spirit is on a preacher, for example, an audience without quite realising it may begin to be affected as God intends them to be. That part in a person which can be open to hypnotism should be open to the control of the Holy Spirit and you will find that with men of outstanding preaching ability such as Finney and Whitefield, vast crowds could come under the control of God. Audiences were caught, so enwrapped in what was said that they lost sight of the immediate surroundings and became taken up with what the preaching described. I think it was Whitefield who on one occasion in the course of preaching so described a storm with its fury and blast that men were going out of the church wrapping their coats around them to step into blazing sunshine! They had been so gripped by the power of the preaching. I seem to recall that when another preacher dramatically described someone approaching a dangerous precipice, a man in the audience was so strongly affected that he interrupted by shouting, 'He's over!' What an influence has the tongue!

We'll move down now from lofty realms to a much more mundane and natural area of life and observe Satan's interest in the tongue. Itself such a little member, but oh! the troubles it can stir. Those of you who are in leadership learn very quickly in the course of your work that the tongue is a divider of people, a sower of discord, a cause of endless trouble. You meet the other side of the hearing situation I described yesterday. Someone passes on a tit-bit of information and it comes back to the first person of whom the thing was spoken. This brings discord and division which may never heal until the wrongdoer humbles himself and apologises honestly. 'Yes, I did say that. I regret it now. I am sorry for the thing I have done.'

Let me tell you something about this kind of thing. When you speak a word or a few sentences it is like a farmer plucking a chicken and letting the feathers fly to the wind. You can never gather them all up again. They are blown hither and thither. Similarly in the moment you say unwise and unkind things about another the words go from you like feathers on the wind. They go from one to another and you can never gather them all up again—that is one danger of spoken criticism and unkindness.

I made a rule as a very young Christian never to speak evil of anybody, simply because I felt the Bible taught this. I am not saying I have kept the rule absolutely in all circumstances but in general I do live by it. I advise you to adopt it. Just don't indulge in evil speaking. If you have something to say about a person, say it directly to him or her if God leads you to do that but don't talk critically to others. I do know, of course, that in leadership there are times when we have to discuss situations and people for their own good but generally that rule still applies. If you know something nasty about a person do not tell others about it. Don't speak evil one of another, and even supposing you know a matter to be true, that in itself is no good reason for spreading it. A thing can be absolutely true and in speaking of it you can be telling no lie, but that doesn't necessarily justify your saying it—no, not for one moment. There is a law of love. Ask yourself the question, 'If the tables were turned would I like people to say this about me?' The answer is, 'No.' Well, apply the golden rule, 'Do unto others as you would that they should do unto you.' Forever recognise the law of love. Don't ask, 'Is the thing I am saying true?' but rather, 'Is it

57

Christ-like? Is it kind? Is it good? Is it wholesome?' You well know that if someone for whom you very deeply care does something foolish you will guard that person. It may be a member of your own family and you know that if his mistake becomes public knowledge things will be very difficult for him. I tell you, you will guard your brother. You will shield him. You will stand between him and the consequences of his folly. You don't blaze the disgrace abroad. You keep it quiet. You act in love because you love your brother. Well, act in this way towards the whole church and to all others.

I know you, probably better than anybody else in this company knows you. I know almost all of you and many of you I know very deeply. What if I began to go round saying, 'You know, I am really shocked at what so-and-so told me. I can hardly believe it. Would you have thought that?' 'Oh no, no.' And, 'You know how much you think of so-and-so. Well, it might interest you to know X, Y, and Z about her. Would you believe it?' 'No, I can hardly believe that.' I could split this company into a thousand fragments overnight and so could many others, but we don't do that. Someone bares his soul to a leader, and the leader should have anointed ears. He should hear as a servant of God and act as Christ would act which is in a totally trustworthy way. Friend, if you hear something to someone's disadvantage do the best you can for him. Don't spread it. Don't multiply trouble. Our forms of public worship may go regularly on but if love has gone from a congregation I think you will find that God has also to a great extent withdrawn His Presence. You will find that much of this kind of trouble comes through the tongue—that unruly member.

We come now to a slightly different level. I am sure you will appreciate that there are many other things which can be fitted into the last category, but you can do that for yourselves at your own convenience. I want to come to other ways in which the tongue can be used, not with the open antagonism and nastiness which is easily recognised—not something you can see coming against which you can prepare but something more subtle, something which is sometimes referred to as the language of women. I am sorry about this, sisters. Now, unfortunately, I can't remember the detail of an article I read on this many years ago but it was a most illuminating and instructive article. It described this kind of situation. One lady addresses another: 'You know, dear, that's a lovely dress you are wearing. I remember noticing it particularly at Jean's wedding—was that two years ago? I can hardly believe it was as much as that. I thought it was most becoming but I see you've changed the hat you are wearing with it. You know, this one suits you so much better. The other one didn't do anything for you at all.' The lady has done nothing but compliment her friend—or has she? I am sure you have heard comments like these. Delightful—quite delightful! You may chuckle. Now that is only a small sample of the female cut and thrust. I do wish I could remember other examples from that article but you will recognise this kind of thing when you next meet it as you mix with the fair sex!

To be a bit more serious on the same kind of line, there is a deceitful way of picking out someone's fault. You don't say to a third party, 'Isn't that a real nasty quality in so-and-so's character?' You say, 'You know I feel there is real potential in so-and-so. Isn't it a pity about that particular weakness he/she is displaying?' The person remembers the particular weakness and forgets the first part of the sentence. It can be passed over in such a seemingly godly fashion, such a nice considerate way, but, in fact, you are cutting to the quick. God knows all about these wriggles and twists. The tongue—the tongue—I am only touching high points as I go along on this theme. You could have many sermons on the tongue. It's so often in use and it can be so powerful for good or evil.

I will change the subject again just a little. At the breakfast table this morning there was a lovely example of the need to keep a guard on the tongue. A joke had come over from Ireland. I don't know where the culprit who brought it is sitting but the shoe's meant to fit so just put it on! I don't mean that the joke was a crude one, but one of you took it to the Highlands and the company to whom it was told all laughed except one gentleman who immediately announced to the company that he would go next door and take his Bible with him. The teller, a very godly girl, was humiliated and learned a valuable lesson. She will be careful in future. The point of this story is simply to instruct you to be careful with what you allow your tongue to speak. In some companies this story might have been totally acceptable—I don't know what the joke was, my friends won't tell me— but obviously in other companies it might prevent the person telling it from having the ear of at least one individual on a serious matter. A standard had been lowered. Watch the reaction of a thing like that on an audience.

I come from a farming background and there are certain stories that quite amuse me and would never upset the farming community but which would upset some town dwellers because the attitudes of the two groups are different. You must always watch that what you say is not something that will later prevent the Holy Spirit from speaking through you effectively to the person or the people concerned. If you've been born with a sense of humour, it's something that you will quite often have to control. I know that you sometimes think I tell funny stories but as an Irishman might say, 'You should hear the ones I don't tell you.' Some of you have got to know me rather well and evidently my lips occasionally quirk just a little and you know that there is something funny there and you don't know whether it is coming out or not. Quite often it doesn't come out because, while it might have an application and a relevance, there may sometimes be something in it that will cause the atmosphere to lighten. I have to be careful and control the words which pass the lips, to control the tongue. Satan is very, very aware of all these nuances. He is very well aware of how he can catch people with the things they say. Have you never been careless and said something and immediately felt a coldness inside as though the Holy Spirit had withdrawn Himself? Immediately there has been an effect from the words that passed over the tongue in a moment of carelessness, in a moment when you have not been on guard. Watch your tongue. Guard it. It is of tremendous importance.

So Satan tries to get control of that vital organ and God for His part has also a particular interest in the same organ. I am not a trained psychologist and I can't give you all the technical language for this, but I do know that when the functions of speech are controlled of God, something of a very deep and significant nature takes place which affects the whole man, the whole being.

In the early stages of human history men decided to band together and build the tower of Babel—they would reach up to Heaven. Man has always been aspiring to reach Heaven in a wrong way and God confused their language. He divided language at that point to make general communication amongst them impossible because their communication was wrong and dangerous. Now God has ever been interested in the control of the tongue, and when you come to Pentecost you find that there is a sense in which Babel is reversed. It is as though He says, 'Now stop keeping your own tongue under your own control and come into another dimension and let your tongue and your being be controlled by Me.' Something of phenomenal significance takes place when the tongue is yielded. In the upper room they were all filled with the Holy Spirit and they all began to speak in tongues. Their Baptism, I take it, was complete when utterance in tongues was given and in this the tongue was not under their own control but under the control of the Holy Spirit.

Now don't for one moment think that speaking in tongues is the end of the matter. Speaking in tongues is like a half-way house to prophecy and inspired preaching. When you are speaking in a tongue it is very easy to concentrate on God and let your tongue continue. You don't need to trouble about language at all. You don't understand the words you use so your thoughts don't go down side tracks, diverted by words whose meaning you know. It is much easier to remain under power in speaking in tongues than it is in your own language, but when you learn how to do that in tongues it is comparatively easy to transfer the ability to your own language, so that when prophesying, for example, you are not distracted by the meaning of the words you speak. You remain concentrated on God and find that His power can come flooding through your tongue in your own language. The process, while in a sense controlled by you, is in a deeper sense controlled by God.

I don't want to go into detail today about the tremendous importance of the gift of prophecy and inspired preaching. These are amongst the highest functions vouchsafed to men. In them men may speak as the oracles of God and we have a duty to represent God to others in the power and demonstration of the Holy Spirit. The gospel ought always to be so preached. Indeed in my view a preacher is not free of the blood of his fellows unless he brings them the gospel in this way.[2]

When a person comes deeply under Divine control as was frequently the case with the late Kathryn Kuhlman, for instance, very wonderful things can happen. Her mind was controlled, her tongue was controlled and revelation gifts came into operation. She spoke of things that she had no way of knowing by any natural means. There came the revelation of God. If we would be really effective preachers we must get to the place where we have no confidence in the flesh but are confident in the Living God alone. We must look to Him for revelation and for utterance. We must have Divine control. It seems almost a truism to say, 'God wants your tongue' but remember God said, 'How shall they hear without a preacher?' It is with the tongue that we communicate. It is in language that we think. God wants us to be at His disposal to spread His word amongst men—not always from platforms but in our everyday meeting with people—in our social contacts. He has not commanded angels to go into all the world and preach the gospel. This privilege has been given to men. Christ told His disciples, 'Ye shall receive power...and ye shall be my witnesses.' 'Tarry until ye be endued with power from on high.' They tarried and they were filled with the Spirit.

Now upon every one of them came a tongue like as of fire. May I remind you again that on the day of Pentecost the symbol of the Holy Spirit was not a flaming head to indicate thought, or flaming shoulders to speak of burden-bearing, nor yet flaming hands to indicate work, nor flaming feet to run with the gospel. It was not even a flaming heart to betoken love. It was a flaming tongue to indicate speech. 'Ye shall be my witnesses.' How does a man witness? with the tongue. There were no exceptions on the day of Pentecost. There was a tongue upon them every one. They were filled with the Holy Spirit and what was the first effect of this of which we read? They all began to speak and they all began to speak in tongues as the Spirit gave them utterance. We do not read that the Holy Spirit began to speak. They did the speaking but He gave the power. The great commission began to be outworked. Poor failing Peter was transformed. He spoke boldly and effectively for Christ that day. No longer afraid of a servant maid, he accused the assembled thousands in Jerusalem of the murder of Christ. Instead of fear dominating him fear fell on them and they came to Christ by the thousand. The Holy Spirit had come and His servants spoke boldly for Him.

Again I am reminded of that lovely story where Christ is pictured in conversation with an archangel on going back to Heaven when His work on earth was done. The archangel was asking about His plans for the establishment of His Kingdom and on learning of the part He had planned for men he exclaimed, 'What, are you trusting them again?' 'Yes,' said Christ, 'I am trusting them again.' Let the words sink in. 'I am trusting them again.' He is trusting you. He is trusting me. Will we be worthy of that trust? Will we be witnesses for Him? I won't belabour the point, but do open your ears to God this morning. Put yourself at His disposal. Let Him both guard your tongue and use your tongue.

And so the two great commanders look on the battlefield. They both seek control of that little part of the body—the tongue. The one who secures that strong point (or weak point) has a tremendous tactical advantage. Never under-estimate the importance to God of the control of the tongue. If He doesn't get control in this area you are going to live, I think, a comparatively ineffective Christian life. As people deepen in God they tend to speak less and less to each other and they also tend to speak less to God. They tend to listen more and they listen more and more to God. Deep saints are seldom garrulous in private. With deepening spirituality there is a withdrawing into a more silent place. I don't want to lay an unnatural burden on any of you or a strain. I am a very natural person myself and there are times I feel perfectly free to talk very fully, but quite often I am drawn into a place of deep quietness and I think this increases with deepening spirituality. Even at a natural level there is often a degree of wisdom in being quiet. I have sometimes quoted to some of you a saying of my old grandmother. She died when she was about 93 and would be about 90 when she came on this *bon mot*. She was delighted with it and I might say rolled it under her tongue. 'It is better to remain silent and be considered a fool than to open your mouth and remove all doubt about it.' Evidently I quoted this to one of my Assistant Heads in school soon after his appointment. It must have found a mark. He certainly reminded me of it in later years and with a good deal of relish too.

So often a company is gathered and some foolish person wants to be the centre of conversation and he talks, talks, talks and tries to dominate a situation. He wants to speak on everything that comes up. He becomes a menace, a nuisance.

For years I chaired an erudite educational committee. There were professors, inspectors, the Depute Director of the Examination Board and other leading educationalists on it. It provided for me a wonderful study in human nature. There was one of them who just couldn't stop talking. He could come in late for a meeting and he seemed to be speaking as he came through the door even if somebody else was holding the floor. He would sometimes speak all the way to his chair, perchance reversing the very things he had advocated at the meeting the month before. He just couldn't keep his mouth shut. On one occasion when he was part of a delegation we failed to achieve our goal because of this weakness. Over-talking lost us the case. The joke is that I can write this quite freely for I don't believe that the person concerned had the slightest idea of his tendency. On that same committee there was another whom I shall name this time (I don't usually name names if my comments are unflattering). He is Dr. John Walker, now Director of the Scottish Examination Board and a life-long personal friend. We were in the same class at University and have been in contact over the years. He would sit in these committee meetings and was quite capable of remaining silent through a whole morning and afternoon session. But you know, when John did speak everybody listened and indeed some-body was quite liable to say, 'John, would you like to put that on paper? That could form the basis of the next piece of work that the committee has to do.' It was so good. It was so well thought-out. It was so profound. He was not a chatterer but when he had something to say he said it and it was effective—the tongue and its influence!

I think I can move on to the next part of the body because my treatment of it will not be very lengthy. I had intended to take the body parts in pairs in any case. The next is the neck/shoulder combination. Now has that surprised those of you who were trying to anticipate things?

When the devil has his way he produces a stiff neck. Remember the stiff-neckedness of the Israelites. The neck and the shoulders are very closely attached—yes, quite! So what does Satan want with those parts apart from your stiff neck (of which he entirely approves)? He wants you to be burdened, deeply, permanently burdened with your own affairs and the affairs of the world. Many of the people I have had to deal with through the years are people who were carrying very heavy burdens on their shoulders, even although Christ had given that wonderful invitation, 'Take my yoke upon you and learn of me, for I am meek and lowly of heart, and ye shall find rest to your souls.' The yoke was laid across the neck and shoulders of oxen. Christ took up the figure and said (I paraphrase) 'Take my yoke on your shoulders and you'll find that my yoke is easy and my burden is light.' Satan places intolerable burdens on human shoulders and people break under them and increase their burdens by their reactions to Satan. They build the load and he makes sure that it presses heavily on them, and they are forever adding to that load by the aggregation of sin and wrongdoing until it becomes quite intolerable—the weight of sin and iniquity and the cares of life. Christ could speak in His own day of the Pharisees who were unwilling to put out a hand to help people upon whom they had laid fearful burdens. They would not help one little bit. They left them with their burdens. Satan will always leave you with your burdens. He is cruel to the utmost degree and it is a great joy to him to see you not only stumbling but falling under your burden and being crushed and broken by it. There's no mercy in Satan. He will use your shoulders and your stiff neck as the place on which he will place his load and you'll carry it on tottering legs until you go down into the grave with it. That's Satan's strategy where your shoulders are concerned.

Now God also has a plan and a strategy. He says, 'Put My yoke upon your shoulders. Don't try to go free. You'll be a prey to Satan if you try to do that. Don't try to be free. Put My yoke upon your shoulders. It will steady you. It will control you. It will prevent you going in wrong directions and My hand will be on the reins.'

Now you folks probably don't know much about the harnessing of horses so let me just say a little about this. Things are a little different in our day from the yoke that was laid across the oxen in Christ's day but the principle is very similar. Take an example from my own early days of a horse being harnessed to a cart. I am not going through all the pieces of the harness, but suffice to say that there was placed over the shoulders a neck collar and to that was attached the chains that were in turn attached to the cart. Over the horse's head there was a bridle and a bit to which reins were attached and the driver of the cart held these reins in his hand. In the case I envisage, a young horse was being broken in. It was really a very painful experience for the animal because, being used to freedom, it chafed under the yoke—this restricting thing round its neck and shoulders. The first thing it often did was to rear right up on its hind legs and kick out with its fore feet. If the farmer was not careful he could be clobbered by those great hoofs but he knew his job and there were usually two men present at such a time, one on each side of the horse. When it reared they rugged it back to the ground. The jerking rope pulled the bit, which hurt the horse's mouth. Being a high-spirited animal a horse often reared up again and again just as you and I do when God puts His bridle on us and we don't like it. Our restriction is painful and we try to get the bit out of our mouths. The horse will try and reject the bit if it possibly can. Ultimately it learns that there is no future in rearing up and it begins to walk along and, oh, horror of horrors, there's a fearful thing trundling and rattling along behind it and it is tied to this thing. It fears this and objects to it thoroughly, so it lashes out with its hind feet and hits solid wood, but being high-spirited it kicks again and again and again. Sometimes if it is a tough horse it kicks a cart to matchwood but ultimately the horse is broken in. See the same horse weeks later: it goes docilely along the road and its driver scarcely needs to touch the reins but controls it with a word, 'Hup!'—turn to the right; 'Vane!'—to the left; a shout to stop or go. It is under control.

Now, the horse is very much happier at this stage than it was at the breaking in stage. If it has a good master it can have a very happy life indeed. He will see that it is never overloaded. He will see that it is well fed and watered and never overworked. There can develop a relationship of affection and love between master and horse and even in the training of a horse, if he is a kindly man, he'll do it in a kindly way. He'll only use enough force to let it understand and then he'll deal far more in affection than he will in harshness. Horses are wonderful animals. They are beautiful creatures, intelligent, and they will respond to love and give life-long loyalty.

I was in a sauna recently and afterwards went into the lounge where the Commonwealth Games were on television. There was horse racing on the screen. I don't have television so this was something I seldom see. The horses were beautiful animals. I don't know how those of you who do have television react to this kind of thing, but I react very strongly indeed to seeing a horse that has run its heart out in a long gruelling race, being flogged over the last twenty yards by a jockey standing in the stirrups, trying to force that last extra effort out of the animal. I don't know why this kind of cruelty is still allowed. The horse has almost run its heart out and it is treated in this way. It is scandalous. You can have a wonderful relationship with a horse—a relationship of love. You can get a tremendous amount from animals if you have a God-like, Christ-like attitude to them. You can draw something out of them that is wonderful, lovely.

Christ says, 'Let Me yoke you. Let Me put My harness on your neck. Let Me take the reins in My hand and guide you and you'll never get more of a burden than you can bear, for My yoke is easy and My burden is light.' And here is a wonderful paradox. The men and women who go into the deepest places of prayer and intercession with God find coming upon them the burden of the world, a share of the burden that came on Christ. There comes a peculiar duality. The burden in one sense doesn't come on them personally. They are not personally unhappy. It comes on a part of the spirit which is tuned to bear it—the intolerable burden of a world's agony coming upon a human and yet at the end of the day the words of Christ remaining true, 'For my yoke is easy and my burden is light,' and they are totally in joy and in agony at the same point in time. You can be personally at peace with God and carrying a fearful burden for others. Again let me remind you of men like Praying Hyde, Father Nash, Rees Howells, David Brainerd—men of prayer. Take Praying Hyde. He carried a fearful load from Christ for his fellow men. He entered at least in some measure into the fellowship of Christ's sufferings. He believed that Christ goes on suffering for us—being touched by the feeling of our infirmities—not indifferent to our needs. Praying Hyde yielded himself to God for a life of intercession and prayer. He willingly let much of normal life pass him by. For Christ's sake he chose a single life and lived sacrificially for God. Surely in his case he gave his shoulders to God. He willingly accepted all the burden God wanted him to bear. Shall we learn from the servants of old? Who is going to have your neck and shoulders? The destroyer, Satan the cruel; or God, the lover of the souls of men? The rival commanders await your decision, not only with regard to the mind, the eyes, the ears, the tongue but now the shoulders as well.

Notes

[1] Slightly abridged.
[2] These matters are developed more fully in my earlier books, particularly *Reflections on the Baptism in the Holy Spirit* and *Reflections on the Gifts of the Spirit*, to which readers are referred.

5

The Heart and the Knees

The parts of the body that I feel God has brought to my mind for this morning are the heart and the knees.

The heart. You may think that of all the parts of the body I have taken this will be the easiest to preach about. Do you know, I have found it to be the one that has the greatest difficulty of all. I don't quite know why, but I found that as I was before God awaiting revelation, the knowledge of how to tackle the subject was long in coming. Think of this first from Satan's point of view—the captivation of the heart. Probably most of us are familiar with God's attitude. He says, 'My son, give me thy heart,' and 'Guard thy heart above all that thou guardest for out of it are the issues of life.' God openly claims the human heart and the love of the human heart, but you will find that Satan in his approach to ordinary people doesn't normally make that claim in any direct way. He doesn't ask for human love. He will demand allegiance if you go far enough along the road of evil and he will ultimately desire worship but at first there is no open demand of that kind. So wherein is his assault on your heart—how does it come? And what does God mean when He says, 'Give me your heart'?

I believe that God seeks a full allegiance which I will be speaking of shortly but there is another aspect of things I would like to examine first. 'Where your treasure is there will your heart be also.' Don't think in terms of just one great love of a person's life as being the only form of heart idolatry. It's not like that. Many people do not have the grand passion about which romantic novels are written. Life's not always like that. There are such kinds of love and there are those kinds of people, but the ordinary man and woman in the street, the ordinary youth, the ordinary boy and girl do not necessarily have something of a world-shaking nature in the sphere of love; and yet I think that perhaps in a particular way we are all caught on this issue, and instead of Satan having had little access he has had tremendous access to human nature relative to the heart. The clue lies in that word, 'Where your treasure is there will your heart be also.' The love of your heart is there, and what, in simple terms, does that mean?

Take a boy, a young boy, and get to know him so well that he begins to talk to you uninhibitedly. You may find that the love of his heart is football and possibly the team which he supports. In some cases you may find it is an addiction, a disease.

I passed through that phase very early and got rid of the worst of it but I so clearly remember my secondary school days. We would be coming home for lunch or returning to school: there was a group of us, four or five, and we would be trotting along. Two of the company were Rangers mad. Now you really need to know somebody that's got the disease to realise just what it is to be Rangers mad. We would run along and one was centre-forward and he was passing the ball to Alec Gillies, who was passing the ball to Big Jock and it was going here and there right along the street—the Rangers' forwards were in action! There was, of course, no ball and the real joke was that the boys concerned weren't great footballers themselves but that was beside the point! They were living football. It was in the warp and woof. Their hearts were there, their thought was there, their imaginations were there. You think I'm laying things on. I'm not, you know. It was just like that and it went on every day.

I remember speaking to Dr Gordon Strachan who once ministered in the east end of Glasgow. His parish was an area that was 'Rangers daft' and he once told me, 'I'll never forget the night that Celtic beat Rangers 5–0. It was the beginning of a terrible decline for Rangers which lasted for several years. That night it was as though the whole community had suffered bereavement. A dark shadow hung over the whole area. It was almost tangible. The unbelievable had happened. Rangers had not only been beaten by Celtic; they had been humiliated by a 5–0 defeat. It was a fate worse than death.' Now if this kind of thing has never been your addiction you won't understand it, but those of you who have been football daft will understand exactly what I mean.

Time passes and sometimes the boy grows up! He may pass out of that phase and come along the road a bit and a variety of things begin to interest him. With some it can be career, and study towards that end. This is normally greatly encouraged by educators and we tend to exploit this natural instinct and in some cases the ambition shuts out almost every other consideration in life. People give themselves to it. They think about it. They dream about it. They build castles in the air. Their hearts are given in that direction. Come along the road a little and you'll find that some go into business, and money-making can have a fearfully addictive effect on a personality. It can warp. It can turn and twist and change. 'The love of money,' the Bible says, 'is the root of all evil' and there is no doubt at all that an undue love for money is an extremely dangerous thing. It catches the affection of the heart. It catches and grips and binds. There are others who go into political careers and their own name, their own standing, their own prominence becomes of tremendous importance. A politician is often a very odd kind of animal—not all politicians but many of them—often very self-centred, very self-seeking. Again, not all—I don't want to be unfair in my remarks—but with some, politics begins to eat up life. I think of one in particular who was deeply called of God in earlier days who is now immersed in politics. I fear that the call of God has been largely brushed aside. 'Where the treasure is there will the heart be also.' Politics can become the first love of the heart and the energies of life pour in there.

I want you to realise I am being totally reasonable. I am not suggesting for a moment that boys should not play football and be interested in football. I am not suggesting for a moment that people should not be interested in careers and work hard to fulfil normal ambition. I am not saying that people should not go into business to make money. I am not saying people should not go into politics. I am not saying any of these things, but I am saying that there is a danger of any one of these things becoming so out of proportion that it becomes an idol: it becomes the main love of the heart.

I have taken a boy as an example but I could equally have taken a girl with her particular types of daydream and ambition and goal, and there is a whole area that I have not yet touched which is the boy/girl relationship. This can go to great depths. Each frequently makes the other the first love of the heart and the focus of the whole attention. I will come back to this later.

Right now I want you to test what I am saying in your own life. I will give you a moment to ponder. What is it you think about when you have nothing you must think about, when your mind is free just to daydream? Where does your thought go? If you answer that honestly, you will know where your real treasure is, and you may even discern something of the influence Satan has on the citadel of the mind. If the answer to the question is anything other than God or things related to Him or things that are good and true and honest, I think you may assume that Satan has at least an influence on a vital part of your being.

I am not going to call you up here to answer the question publicly one by one, either randomly or otherwise. It would be embarrassing both to you and to the company and it might even tempt you to tell lies and I wouldn't want to be responsible for that. You see, I know human nature reasonably well.

The things that lie in the heart of man.... Exceedingly corrupt is the human heart, desperately wicked; who can know it?

Any one of the things I have mentioned earlier can become very strong indeed if it swings out of control, but the one with which we are probably most familiar is the affection associated with personal human relationships. We tend to forget the other kinds of things of which I have been speaking and the moment the subject is mentioned the mind tends to swing to love relationship amongst humans, and about this we can become very confused.

The place for human affection.... There is no ban on human affection. There is no virtue in an asceticism that is unnatural. Affection in a parent/child relationship is vital. There is a great deal of virtue in handling children. I have so often told that story of the two institutions where orphan children were left: a small one in which they were given family care, a large one where they were treated as mere units. In the larger the mortality rate was much higher than might have been expected and the I.Q. was very much lower than average, whereas in the smaller one where the children were given love and personal affection, where they were held and handled and loved, the mortality rate was very low and the I.Q. was very high. In other words they responded to love; children should be loved; they should be shown love. It should be demonstrable love and they should be encouraged to return love. Affection is a natural thing; it is unnatural not to have it—affection within the family, affection amongst friends, a general attitude of love. Indeed the Bible makes it very clear and plain that love is of God. We should love God and we should love all men. There are different types of love and there is generally no danger in family love unless it turns to a kind of family worship which can become idolatrous. When it is a case of, 'My family is more important than other families and should have special treatment...' things are out of order. There is a worship that is wrong but, in general, family love is in order and should be strongly encouraged. That's not where the greatest danger lies. The danger is more likely to arise with romantic love.

The notion of romantic love in the Western world has been greatly fuelled by literature and more recently by film and television. Love is not regarded in quite the same way in Scripture, or indeed in many other cultures, and yet I feel that there is in romantic love much that is natural and indeed God-given. Don't regard it as a wrong thing. God works through nature and people who are compatible may have a natural attraction to each other. This is often quite spontaneous. That does not mean, of course, that it should always be followed. Inclinations may be natural but that does not mean that they are always right. On the romantic side of life you'll find that probably marriage is possible between an individual and maybe one in a thousand of the population. A natural attraction is not something that is felt towards only one person although people in love would often like to think so. That is not how men and women are basically built. A person may feel an attraction and be aware of the attraction but that is not necessarily a green light to follow the matter any further. The attraction is not the only element to be considered in the formation of a relationship and here people should be careful, because when love is once stirred and is allowed to take a deep grip in a person's heart it is not a tide that is easily turned and the consequences can remain for a lifetime. If you are once deeply attracted to a member of the opposite sex and you yield to the attraction and commit yourself to the other, you cannot by an act of the will simply stop the process. Love grips and the grip can be very deep. If it turns out that a relationship is not in the will of God, a true disciple must submit. God may intervene with the simple word, 'No,' and the person knows it at a deep level of being and may have all the agony of reversal. It may be shown through circumstances that marriage will not be possible and one may be left with all the burden of it, all the pain of it and for some people that can last for a lifetime. I knew of one man—all the participants in this are dead now—who deeply loved a lady who did not return his love but married another. They were all Christians and all belonged to the same Christian fellowship, although fortunately to different local churches. Do you know that many years afterwards they attended a wedding and the man, although himself now married to another, was unable to sit beside the lady? It was too painful. The passion of his early years had never totally passed. He had committed himself to a terrible depth. I felt deeply sorry for that man. I could understand that agony. He had made a commitment and it had never been reversed within him. This is an area in which it is unwise ever to commit yourself until you know the will of God.

Frequently the commitment is not altogether to a person but can sometimes be an externalising or projection of one's own personal ideal. You have your own standard, and you fit that to the person to whom you are attracted. You may try to create a new person. You love not the person he or she is but an ideal person vested with qualities with which you have yourself endowed him/her. This can be a very dangerous thing to do because early or late there will come the awakening. That is not the real person at all. That person was a person of your own imagination, of your idealisation. One day you come to earth with a fearful bump and you can no longer deceive yourself. You have fallen in love with your own reflection in another life, and probably the finer you are the more you idealise and the more awful is the awakening when it comes.

Now supposing an attraction is of God and is right and in His will and is intended to lead to marriage, what then? Well, Satan is still interested—in fact he is probably particularly interested to intervene in what is basically a good and a God-ordained thing. He would give it his own twist and ruin that which in itself is right. He comes in and distorts things and takes people away from the proper God-centred position. You will find that in very few cases do people manage to meet the Divine demand that Christ should receive the full flood of human love and that every other love should pass through Him.

I come now to a part of the teaching that is highly unpopular. Very few people assimilate it or even attempt to obey it but it remains a Divine commandment. It is the law of the New Testament. We for ever seek direct relationships. It is human nature so to do. He is *my* husband. She is *my* wife. She is *my* daughter. He is *my* father—my, my, my— and yet God in Christ has made it very, very plain indeed, 'Thou shalt love the Lord thy God with all thy heart,' and Christ said, 'He that loveth father or mother more than me is not worthy of me.' Indeed He speaks of hating father and mother to point His message although He obviously doesn't want you to hate them in one sense of that word. He does, however, want you to see the relative position in which they should be held. Your relationship should pass through Christ and that is not an easy thing to accomplish.

Nobody taught me this but God. I remember being taught it when my eldest daughter was a toddler and a choice lay before me either to take the attitude, 'She is my child (I am not leaving her mother out of it but I am talking of my own particular relationship)—my daughter. I have a right to love her directly and to regard her as mine,' but God said, 'No,' and I sacrificed that child in the depth of my spirit to Christ and I received her back at a far higher level with a far deeper love. I did the same with the others, and today the bonds that are between us are such that it is a tremendous joy to me and has been through all the years. The relationships are far, far deeper, far, far stronger than if there had been the cloying 'me, my, mine' attitude. Everything has gone through Christ. Every touch goes through Christ and instead of losing my daughters I have gained immeasurably. This, in my view, is the law of God for every human relationship. Touch nobody directly. Let love pass through God. Enjoy the overflow in every relationship that God gives.

Many of you are not going to obey this and I believe that in some of your hearts right now you are saying, 'No, I will have nothing to do with that.' But I tell you if you take the other course you are going to have burned fingers and sore hearts because there is nothing in any human per se which will endure. Indisciplined human loves are often ravished with jealousies and pain and disappointment and people let you down. You may think this is terribly cynical, but really there's no human who is worthy of trust in an absolute sense. I have many friends in this company whom I trust very deeply, relatively speaking. I know them and they know themselves and I know me and I know that apart from Christ we all have breaking points. My code may not always be their code and their code may not be my code, and there is wrapped up in that bundle a time bomb because the moment comes when a code is breached and a trusted person seems to have feet of clay on that point and we disappoint each other. You have a family—and your children go their own way. They let you down and they break your heart. If your love is idolatrously tied up in family or on anything on earth, it is usually only a matter of time before the disappointments come. God's demand is that we be every one rooted and grounded in Him: that no matter what waves roll across our seas, no matter what disappointments at human levels come, we can say, 'By Thy grace I go on—I go on.' They all forsook Christ and fled but He went on. He didn't utter a piteous cry about what they had done to Him. He saw beyond human defection and 'He endured as seeing Him who is invisible.' He was rooted and grounded in God. His heart's affection was in the right place. He loved all men and He loved them passionately but He was not bound by any or crippled by any human relationship. Did Peter deny Him with oaths and curses? did even John flee ultimately? did they all forsake Him? None of these things defeated Christ: 'He endured as seeing Him who is invisible.'

Through the various crises of life I have known my own dark waters. I have known pains and griefs but I have also known that there stood by me One, not merely like the Son of God, but the One who is the Son of God. In the crisis hours He has come to me and spoken to my spirit and by His grace I have always been able to go on. I have felt as though the world was crumbling. My life seemed in jeopardy but always Christ came. It was like the shining of a star. The light spread and the rift in the clouds opened and I was able to go through. And you don't come through maimed with the feeling, 'Oh what has happened to me? I've got a wounded leg and it will never be right and I'll go limping all my life.' There is a sense in which you do go limping all your life like Jacob, but it is a limp that causes you to lean on the Son of God and you come out into glory. You don't come out into a half light and say, 'Oh God, that was a terrible thing that happened.' You come out into a new day with the shining and blazing splendour of the Son of God in victory, not in half victory/half defeat, but in triumph through God. I plead with you—never have any foundation in your life save Christ. If you do, your ship will one day be battered on the rocks. There is no way round this. There is no way over it. There is no way under it. I believe God allows trouble to come into every life which knows this truth but does not follow it. In His kindness and His love He sometimes allows stark tragedy to bring you into His reality. We journey on into eternal truth and there can be no deviation. Truth lives on and there is no other way that will endure. If in your earth life you play the fool it has all got to be undone. There's no future in folly. There's no future in wrong ways and wrong attitudes. There's only one way—'I am the Way, the Truth and the Life'—and the principles I am teaching this morning are eternal principles—difficult for a man ever to receive if his heart is in the grip of the wicked one, and Satan has stormed the citadels of most human hearts and he has his troops firmly embedded in those citadels. You may not be aware of his entities and I'm not speaking of demon possession at the moment but of the influence of evil forces. You may think your thinking is your own and the result of your own attitude and reasoning when, in fact, you are in the grip of another, and you may never know how deep that grip is until you seek freedom and you may never know the joy of freedom until you experience it. You never know how deep bondage is until the bondage is broken. Satan knows well that word of God, 'Guard thy heart above all that thou guardest for out of it are the issues of life.' These are God's words, not mine. Satan knows the truth of this and he attacks the citadel of the heart ruthlessly and relentlessly. He will try to take you down through the loves of the heart.

But God looks at the citadel and He gives you the teaching that I have given you this morning: 'My son, give me thy heart.' Let Me be your first choice—'Give Me your heart.'

Now I think I said that after considering the two sides I would then for a moment look at Christ, look at the heart of Christ. Why is it that we all instinctively trust Christ? What is it about Christ that causes this?

Someone came for an interview this morning. It was urgent and very interesting. The person concerned had a problem but was afraid that God's answer might not be the one that was desired. What do you do in a case like that? Well, first of all you recognise honesty. God likes honesty. I don't like a person to come to me and to tell me too glibly, 'Oh, yes, I'll do whatever the Lord says.' That comes from the lips, and deep down in the heart the person sometimes has no intention of taking God's way if it is not the way he or she wants; but when a person comes and says, 'I am afraid to know the will of God in case it is not what I want and I am not quite sure that I will be able to do such and such,' I feel there is hope for such a person. Now the case in question proved to be really a lovely case. The person became quite definite. Had Christ been present in the flesh she would have asked Him what she should do. She really did want to know what Christ wanted her to do. What most of us are afraid of is perhaps not so much knowing the will of God as not being sure of it and fearing that we may go further in denying ourselves over a matter than He is asking, and on the other hand we are afraid not to take action in case He *is* demanding it. It is often the area of uncertainty that causes the real trouble. I took this lady, who confessed her unwillingness to go all the way with God, to the point where she was willing to be made willing. It then became quite clear that she really did want to know the will of God and that if she knew His will she would obey it. Actually what she really wanted was me to tell her what to do, but God didn't tell me what she should do. She had asked a trusted friend to tell her what she should do prior to this and, very wisely, he did not tell her either. I think that may have caused a little disappointment but I advise you never to let such a response or lack of it be a disappointment. Be careful of the person who tells you too readily what you should do. There are too many people who will tell you very freely what to do when they have no real guidance from God and it isn't their business.

If you had a beloved child would you send all your messages to your child through a Nanny? Would you not want to speak to the child yourself? Would you not want the child to speak to you? Well, God never made me a Nanny-goat! There are times when God wants to speak directly to His children with nobody between.

There are times of course when I have clear revelation and know it. That is all in order but do be careful of people who are too quick to tell you what the will of the Lord is. I reckon that if the Lord wants to let me know His will, well, He knows where I stay! That doesn't mean that I don't receive advice and sometimes the will of the Lord through another—don't misunderstand me—but don't erect this into a system. I understand that in some groups dependence on others can run to a fearful extreme. Be wary of people who try to take over the direction of your life. Appreciate people to whom God has given a spiritual responsibility for you—people who take your hand and reach out and put your hand in the hand of Christ so that a relationship with Him develops. Avoid all personality cults. Avoid the idea that you cannot grow spiritually unless you grow spiritually through me, whoever 'me' might happen to be. Let leaders be aware of the danger of drawing people to themselves. Always draw others to Christ and you will find there is wisdom in that at the end of the day. Perhaps I should say a little more on this theme.

When a true spiritual leader is used in leading a person to Christ a father/son relationship may come into being. The father has a care for the child and has a proper oversight over the new convert. He is in a position to advise and ought to do so—but his goal should never be to draw the convert to himself and make him dependent on himself. He ought always to point beyond himself to God. He should quickly have the other feed directly from God. At the beginning there can be a proper leaning of one on the other but there should come a definite weaning. At this point where the bonds between the two might be expected to slacken the reverse is true. They deepen—but they pass through Christ and true independence in Christ is established.

I remember hearing of a brother being approached by another who wanted to become his spiritual adviser and director. After a little time the first asked what advantage there would be in this. 'Well,' said the latter, 'you need a covering. You need somebody to stand between God and you to give an account in a day to come as Paul indicated in the case of others.' 'Show me your hands,' said the first; the other did so. 'Yes,' said my friend, 'just as I thought. You are an impostor. The only man who will ever stand between God and me has nail prints in His hands.' That ended the matter.

Now I don't want to leave a wrong impression. There is a place for true shepherding. It should go on in every true church. Flocks need shepherds—but they need shepherds who will not lord it over them—but take them beyond themselves to Christ. There are those who truly watch as those who will give account for the souls of others—but this does not imply a master/disciple relationship of rigid control by the former. It envisages a loving heart bearing the burdens of another and leading him in the ways of Christ. It does not envisage a *personal* control or lordship of one life over another.

So my advice to the person referred to earlier was: 'Be in the meetings. Open your spirit. Realise you can never improve on the will of God for your life. Try to recognise and get over the psychological problem because if you feel you are not willing, you are giving yourself a shadow right away. Seek the point of willingness, be totally open and let God bring His peace on you. This will come when you are taking the right road. Don't get agitated and don't get psychologically tripped.'

The heart of Christ—why is it we all trust Him? Immediately she trusted Him—oh yes. If He had been there she would have asked Him. She really wanted to know and she would have accepted whatever He said. Well, He was there, although not in the flesh. What is it about Christ that we trust? Totally loving, totally firm, totally kind, totally pure —He is just Christ. The heart of Christ—the most loving heart in all the world for all men. Never in a wrong relationship with any, never bound, always free, all perfect and then the awful and wonderful part—He wants us to be like Him, to grow into the maturity of the sons of God and to have hearts like His own heart, bearing burdens of a world without a thought of self. There you have it. The battle for the heart—a point of strength or a point of weakness. There are the rival commanders. 'Let me,' says Satan, 'steal your heart.' 'My son,' says God, 'give me your heart.' And you frail sons and daughters of dust are in the central position where you say yes and no. To say nothing is to commit yourself in the wrong direction because we read, 'The whole world lieth in the wicked one,' and your heart begins with having in it the seeds of corruption. God comes and gives you an opportunity to come up higher through the avenue of love.

Now we'll deal with the knees. Actually the two are very

closely linked—I mean the heart and the knees—and I can be very brief on the subject of the knees. I imagine you are wondering what I'm going to say about them. What do you think the devil is going to say about knees? In dealing with faces and lips and ears I might speak of all the modern methods of attempting to beautify them, but the knees! Well, mostly they are reasonably covered although when I was a bit younger, in the days of mini skirts, I might have had quite a lot to say about them, but they are reasonably concealed these days. What do you reckon is the interest of the wicked commander in the knees?

The thought behind knees in my mind this morning is kneeling, worshipping and, from his point of view, idolatry. The Bible has a great deal to say about idolatry. It was a curse that ran through the ages. Men made idols of gold and silver and brass and precious metals and many other things. In heathen lands they still make them and bow down to them. Westerners tend to be contemptuous, not realising that behind idolatry there often lies demonology. That's why the priests of Baal were so surprised when there was no answer to their cry to the heathen gods when confronted by Elijah. Normally there would no doubt have been answers: there was real power moving behind the idols. Paul could teach that when men sacrificed to idols they were sacrificing to the demons that lay behind the idols. For that reason, eating food sacrificed to idols was forbidden and, of course, with enlightenment, idolatry died out of the land and overnight it died out of the human heart—or did it? Indeed no! You see idols are not confined to grotesque manufactures of human hands, to outward emblems, grotesque figures and so on. Idolatry is a matter of the heart and it is deep-rooted in the heart. I can be brief about this by referring to the heart since we have already studied it. In Satan's attempt to grip the human heart much of what I said applies to things which become idols—things which begin to be worshipped, and these can be very varied. Call to mind matters we have already considered. See how things can become idols—business, pleasure, sport etc. People begin to worship at their shrines. So idolatry lives on and Satan still aims in this sense at the knees.

Occasionally I preach a sermon on 'The Unreasonableness of God.' There are things that God sometimes asks a person to do which, from a human point of view, seem totally unreasonable. You may not assume that what He wants of you is His rule for everybody. Beware of making these things into a system because that would be very wrong. God has spoken to you in a crisis hour. You know it is His voice. The thing seems totally unreasonable and well nigh impossible but He has spoken and the word is inescapable.

I remember in the life of one lady present now, there came, in early years, a call from God. It involved giving up a long-standing friendship with another girl with whom she had been friendly for years. She had turned to God and He was moving deeply in her life. I thought she was going much too far and that what she was doing was unreasonable. I have, however, lived to learn that what she did was absolutely the commandment of God. God came into that life in a wonderful way as a consequence of the step she took.

I remember a crisis hour in my own life. I was in fifth year in school and was very keen on sport. It had really become an idol to me. I lived on a farm and there was a very flat field just in front of the house where I'd go after school every night and train rigorously. I was particularly good at certain distances. I had been placed for Scotland both in running and in jumping. I held the school high jump record for several years. These things had become idols and I hadn't quite realised it. At this time I was also seeking God. My life was at a crisis point. I had just won the school high jump and the county sports were due. There was a gold medal for winning the high jump in these and my heart was set on that gold medal. I really wanted it but God spoke to me. He spoke to me from a hymn book one Sunday and what He said didn't suit me one little bit. I quickly flicked over the page. I wanted a different kind of word. You know how you try to trick yourself when God speaks to you and you don't want to hear. The next word was just as definite as the first, maybe more so. I couldn't escape it. One line read, 'Renounce every idol, no matter how dear.' Suddenly before my spirit came the thought that that gold medal in hell would have very little significance. My life was at a turning point. Now I'm not saying I would have gone to hell but that is how it came to my mind. It broke me. It broke me completely. I couldn't escape. I felt God was speaking deep in my heart and I clenched my teeth and said, 'All right, I'll do it,' but it was costly, very costly. I had to go to the P.E. teacher who was, I imagine, a militant agnostic if not an atheist. He held strong left wing views and was not sympathetic to religion. I had to go in and say, 'Sir, I'm not going to take part in the county sports.' I had been entered for the high jump and a relay race. 'What do you mean?' Now teachers were teachers in those days, really authoritarian. I said, 'Well, I don't feel I can take part.' 'Why can't you take part?' So I explained to him the religious background and my strong conviction. It was an awful hour. I'll never forget it but I stuck to my decision. He indicated that if I didn't run in the relay race I would let others down and that I really had an obligation. I said, 'All right, I'll accept that.' I felt free in my spirit to do this. I didn't want to let anybody down. I declined, however, to take part in the jump—the thing my heart had been set on. The boy whom I had beaten in the school sports won the gold medal.

That, you may feel, was an extremely unreasonable thing and yet it was in my life a critical thing. You may feel it was a very unreasonable thing for Liddell, the great Olympic record breaker, to refuse to run on a Sunday, but whether you agree or disagree with his view about the Sabbath, you cannot but respect the character of the man who would not run because he felt it to be wrong. You will sometimes find that God is ruthless in dealing with idols.

I want you to realise that through many years I have encouraged school pupils to take part in sport, to have high jumps and long jumps and many other kinds of event. I'm not suggesting that these things are wrong in themselves, but in a person whose life God wanted, these things had got right out of proportion. God wanted to control my life and He disciplined me and broke my idol.

You will know the idols that are in your lives, the things where you have secret groves and your places of worship.

I will pass on quickly. What is God's interest in your knees? The attitude of prayer, of intercession, the attitude of worship, submission to the Divine. I suppose some of the happiest moments that humans have ever known on earth have been on their knees. The more deeply people know God the more time they generally spend on their knees.

I remember one of you who is here this morning, who once had a vision of God's plan in her life in relation to the throne of God. It was a hidden place of prayer, something which had in it no appeal whatever to the flesh. In my view the ministry of intercession is one of the greatest ministries that is ever committed into the hands of men. By it, nations are changed, revivals occur and God is glorified. The place of intercession.... Once again I urge you to read of Praying Hyde, of Rees Howells, of Finney and Father Nash. Read the diaries of David Brainerd and you may be persuaded that prayer is vital and indispensable in spiritual warfare. Find the place of prayer and intercession—on your knees before God. Real prayer, not mere words, but intercession that changes men and nations.[1]

Who will have your knees? Satan, with all the idolatry of

the human heart, or God, with all the potential for advancement of the Kingdom of God?

Note

[1] For further comment on the importance of prayer and intercession I refer you to two of my other books: *Reflections on the Gifts of the Holy Spirit* and *The Clash of Tongues: with Glimpses of Revival*—chapters on faith in the first and the testimony of Mary MacLean in the second.

6

The Hands and the Feet

The points in the body with which I have dealt, points in which both Satan and God are interested, are the mind, eyes, ears, tongue, shoulders and neck. Yesterday I took the heart and the knees and I know that there has been speculation amongst you as to what the final two will be on this last morning. I won't go through the whole list of the speculations you have made but two of these interested me. One was the Achilles tendon and the other was the backbone. I would like to make very brief comments about both of these before I come to my own theme.

The Achilles heel is actually a point of particular interest. It reminded me of that word which warns about 'the sin that doth so easily beset' and I imagine that we all have one area or another where we are particularly vulnerable. I presume many of you will know the derivation of the phrase. It comes from Greek mythology. As a babe, the mighty warrior Achilles was supposed to have been dipped in the River Styx, making his body invulnerable to all kinds of attacks. As he was being dipped, however, his nurse held him by one heel and as a result the heel was not covered by the preserving liquid. Ultimately he died as a result of an arrow wound in this one vulnerable part. There may be in a character great strength and great powers of resistance but also a point of particular vulnerability, an Achilles heel. Of course, Satan is very well aware of this and again and again he brings his attack to bear on the one point of supreme weakness. And God also is aware of the position and He would strengthen the life on that particular point. He is a wise man who recognises his Achilles heel, not taking the proud attitude, 'Oh, I am all right. Nothing like that would affect me,' but being humbly aware of the points where he is vulnerable and can be brought down.

I don't think I need to specify in detail the areas in which we are particularly prone to defeat. You can fill in the blanks yourself. You know that point where he gets you down again and again and again—the point at which you feel you have almost no armour, no resistance.

In my own case, I remember being very well aware in early years of such an Achilles point and I will never forget the consequence of the Baptism in the Spirit. I discovered that when the next arrow came that would normally have pierced the Achilles heel it dropped to the ground as though it had met a wall of fire around me leaving me unscathed. The Baptism in the Spirit was of tremendous significance to me in many ways and in this vital area it gave me power to resist in a way I had never experienced before. Thank God, there is a covering for every Achilles heel.

The second of the additional points—the backbone. You may say, 'In what way is the devil interested in the backbone and in what way is God?' In a nutshell Satan is keen to take away any backbone you've got and leave you with nothing but gristle—a spineless fushionless creature, but God is both minded and able to give you a backbone of steel. If you have no backbone when you come to Him He will surely put you through processes that will develop one.

One of the things about Christianity which has always

appealed to me is the fact that it really does change people. I don't believe that there is much change in human personality in normal circumstances. The foundations of character are formed early and fundamentals rarely change but Christianity does change people fundamentally. It can take a person with an extremely bad temper and alter him. It can take away the bad temper. God really does change deep things in us. He can take a person who is weak, and strengthen the character and change the personality. In preaching I frequently say, 'If you have no backbone when you come to Christ you will find that Christ will give you one.' And He does. He strengthens and changes character. The devil on the other hand takes away the backbone from his dupes and gives a substitute. He can give a stubbornness, a rebelliousness and a hardness that may appear to be strength but which, in fact, is ultimately found to be weakness. So if you feel that you suffer from lack of backbone Christ will come in on that level too.

Now we'll leave these extra parts of the body that have been suggested and move to the two that I am particularly concerned with this morning. First the hands—I am not sure that you will get a proper idea of the importance of hands if you don't for a moment think of what life would be like without them. We take so many things for granted—so many parts of the body don't seem particularly important until something goes wrong. The back is a good example. You are scarcely aware of the functions it performs until something goes wrong with it. Then you suddenly realise how important your back really is. Take your big toe. You are hardly aware of its existence, but drop a heavy weight on it and you will realise just how important that forgotten member really is. First you will find that you can't put the normal weight on your foot so to save the toe you will tend to walk on the side of the foot. That throws other things in your leg out of alignment and you go limping along the road and things get worse and worse. That big toe is far, far more important than you realised.

Now with the hands, just think of what life would be like without them. In fact, if the whole world found themselves handless overnight there would be mass death because there are so many things we just can't do without the use of our hands. I know people can be trained to use feet and so on, but if it came suddenly, the consequences would be fearful and fatal. So we agree from the beginning that hands are vitally important. Hands signify the things that we do and they are one of three parts of the body to which Christ particularly referred in one context:

> And if thy hand cause thee to stumble, cut it off: it is good for thee to enter into life maimed, rather than having thy two hands to go into hell, into the unquenchable fire. And if thy foot cause thee to stumble, cut it off: it is good for thee to enter into life halt, rather than having thy two feet to be cast into hell. And if thine eye cause thee to stumble, cast it out: it is good for thee to enter into the kingdom of God with one eye, rather than having two eyes to be cast into hell; where their worm dieth not and the fire is not quenched (Mark 9:43–48).

The eye—the things that you see; the hand—the things that you do; the foot—the places where you go. If any of these activities come between your soul and God to the point of taking you away from Christ you are better to cast off the offending member than to keep it and find the hell that goes with it. The hand comes into this category. As Satan looks at this vital part of the body he brings his batteries against it to make a breakthrough into your life and personality. He wants to control the things that you do; he wants your hands employed in his service. He wants you to be active for him.

I am aware that in a company like this people have no wish to offer themselves to Satan in the way that is done in black magic and witchcraft circles where people deliberately offer themselves into his hand for his service. That is at the extreme end of the spectrum, and I am not spending time on that. The temptation to you and the form of Satanic attack are really quite different. He wants to engage you in things which are off-beam, things that are wrong but do not seem *very* wrong since you are unlikely to be tempted by things that are obviously evil. You have your standards, you have your code and there are certain things you would not do, certain lines you would not cross. 'I wouldn't want to take a job with that company. I wouldn't like to be involved in any direct way in gambling, or in the liquor trade. I would keep my hands off that kind of thing.' You don't want an involvement that offends your code even although it is not evil to the degree that you might judge witchcraft to be. Now Satan doesn't particularly attack on these issues because by and large you don't *have* to work in the distillery trade; you don't *have* to work in a gambling office. There are other avenues of employment. It's not so much that he catches you in this kind of way but he comes rather to things that you couldn't really categorise as wrong. They are peripheral and unimportant in themselves but they occupy your time and attention and you become wrongly involved in them. They become central to your life. Thus he diverts your attention from the things of God and has you fill your hands with things that are of no real value or consequence in the eternal world. He is anxious for you to have many things in your hand that may in their proper place be perfectly right, but he wants you to have them out of proportion until they distort your life. They assume a false importance and take your time and attention. Basically he wants to fill your hands; to fill them to such an extent that they have no room left for the things of God. He wants your life to be so full that God will be excluded or at least not fully served.

Perhaps I should give a concrete illustration. I remember

once praying with a brother who was seeking his Baptism and after receiving it he told me of four specific things God asked him to do before he received. One of these referred to work. Being good at craft work he started a small manufacturing side-line in addition to his normal job. God wanted that life in His service and He quite clearly asked him to give up the side-line. This he did and was soon using his spare time unsparingly in God's service. The manufacturing business was not wrong. It was not sinful to make leather bags and fancy goods—but for him it was not expedient. God wanted his time and energy.

Satan will settle for you not being positively active in his kingdom. He will even settle for you not being involved in definitely wrong things. He will settle for you being so engaged in things that are not the things of God that you have no time left, and no energy left, for the work of God. That is a very wise strategy from his point of view. It is very easy to catch people. 'You must make a living. You must prepare yourself for making a living. You are a natural person. You have a natural body. It needs recreation and you need to attend to its needs and its wants.' All of these things are perfectly natural and you can't easily argue against them but before you know where you are your whole activity can be diverted to things in which God has no part or place.

Think for a moment on the division of your normal day, starting with the time that you rise. How do we spend a day? According to our temperaments there are those who get up early and have a leisurely breakfast and they go out in a respectable manner, and there are those who get up and they are out within about three minutes flat. There is neither breakfast nor much else. They are buttoning their coats as they run down the street! There are others, of course, who feel that hair is very important and take rather a long time to get it just right. I'm not going to enlarge unduly on this but if you take the total amount of time in a day spent on dressing, eating, reading newspapers, etc., and add to this the time spent at work and in leisure you will find that the whole day can pass with God having had none, or very, very little of it unless a very definite attempt is made to prevent this. You can all think of your own normal daily calendar. Is it consistent with the command to love the Lord our God with all our hearts, souls and minds? He is to have the first of our love and devotion. We may find that our hands are filled with so many things that in many cases God has, in fact, almost nothing.

Stand back and think for a moment—what are we working for? Nearly all of our time is spent in relation to our bodies which will very shortly go back to dust and very little is spent in relation to that eternal part of us that will live for ever. Christ spoke of laying up treasure in Heaven. We should work for and to that end and yet the Christian world largely lives to and for earthly ends and sends comparatively little up to the bank of Heaven. Satan successfully attacks our hands, our actions, the things that we do.

Now God is also interested in our hands. He wants to use them in His service. He wants us to be active in His service. So we come to God and we say, 'Lord, here am I with all my gift, all my talent, all my training and all my ability. I want to work for you,' and God looks down and He says, 'But I don't want you to work for Me.' And that is rather a staggering reception right at the beginning. There you come, bright-eyed and bushy-tailed to be good boys and girls to work for God and God says, 'I don't want you to work for Me,' and that is rather a bump. You say, 'Do you mean that?' Yes, I mean that! God doesn't want you to work for Him. God isn't impoverished. God isn't in that kind of need. God doesn't want any help from you. God doesn't need any help from you. 'Oh, but I thought I was important,' and God says you are not important (in this sense). Get this sorted out right away. You are not important. You can't give God anything. 'But, Lord, I've got a lovely voice. I could sing to the people for You. I could really touch the chords of their hearts.' 'But I don't want you to sing for Me. I don't want you touching the chords of the people's hearts. I don't want you to do anything at all. I don't want you to give anything to anybody.' 'But, Lord, you make me feel terribly insignificant and unimportant.' 'Yes, indeed, that is what I mean to do—to make you feel just exactly that. You are nothing and you have nothing and you'll never be anything or anybody so just settle for it.' 'Well then, Lord, I might as well be dead.' 'Yes, exactly; that's exactly what I want you to be—dead.' 'Oh!'

> My hands were filled with many things,
>   That I did precious hold,
> As any treasure of a king's,
>   Silver, gems or gold.
> The Master came and touched my hands.
>   I must have empty hands, said He,
>   Wherewith to work My works through thee.

'I don't want your hands under your control. I want your hands under My control. Totally empty of the devil's doings, totally empty of your own doings; totally at My disposal. I want your hands. I want to control your whole life. I want you to be dead to self that Christ may be alive and work within you.'

I really don't understand why so few people ever seem to find some of the deep secrets of inner spiritual life. I don't know whether it is the pride and the stubbornness of the human heart, or the darkening of the mind by Satan. I don't understand it, but if you care to read closely the lives of men and women who have been really deeply used—and I mean miraculously used —of God, people like Kathryn Kuhlman or David Wilkerson, you will find that they come to a point of total nothingness. I am almost ashamed to repeat this kind of thing—I do it at every Camp—I do it again and again and again because it is of absolutely critical importance. Wilkerson coming to the end of his tether in the hall in New York when the gangs were surging and mayhem was about to break out—he knew he was at the end of his tether and his inner spirit cried to God and the Holy Spirit came. He had empty hands in that moment. Previously they held various things. He had a soloist who would woo the audience—well, she did, but not in the way he had hoped. He had this and he had that, and he was a good man and he was doing very well, but a good man had to be shown of God that he had no part in the ultimate action. He was finished. The soloist went off the stage and the gangs were erupting, ready for blood and scandal. Then the Holy Spirit came and there came with Him a silence, a sense of control, and then the tears came. The gang leaders went down under the mighty hand of God and God did what Wilkerson could never do.

I have been reading a book about Kathryn Kuhlman, in which she makes this principle very clear. No thought of her own, no action of her own, no anything of her own, but the coming of the Holy Spirit, the anointing of God, the control of the mind—the control of the tongue—the total control by the Holy Spirit. She has clearly enunciated something I have long believed and I'm not sure that I have ever seen another author speak of it in quite the same way.

There came an hour in my life when I noticed for the first time the connection between two truths:—the Holy Spirit coming down on Christ on Jordan's banks and Christ, the Holy One of God, working His miracles by the power of the Holy Spirit. If He was dependent on the Holy Spirit where do we stand? How can we hope to work the works of God in our own strength?

Now don't just let that pass off lightly. This is deep truth that is seldom preached and little recognised. Deference, lip deference, is paid to it but it doesn't often enter into the deeps of the spirit. When it does, a preacher can literally be thrown on to the Holy Spirit. He becomes truly dependent on the moving of the Holy Spirit. I tell you, when He comes in a particular way He can sweep across a company like this and accomplish more in one minute than men could do in a thousand lifetimes. He doesn't deal with men the way men deal with men. There comes that grip, that conviction, that certainty, that choice, and a soul goes up into glory or down into night. The action of the Holy Spirit. And God says, 'I want your hands empty, and I want your hands to be God-filled. I want Christ to control these hands. I want your hands to become the hands of Christ.'

I told you I would point you ultimately to Christ in each of the cases we take and I point you to Christ now. The hands of Christ—have you ever thought about the hands of Christ? Gentle, with an infinite gentleness, caring hands, loving hands, strong hands. No weakness in the hand shake, no aggression in the hand shake; firmness, peace, gentleness radiating from the hands. Hands that stoop down and take the water and towel and wash the disciples' feet. Hands from before whose fingers death fled. He stopped the bier—and there are some who try to maintain that it was wrong according to Jewish Law to touch a dead body. As John McNeill so beautifully put it, 'Christ never touched a dead body; death fled from before His fingers.' The hands of Christ. Hands are really very significant things—a great deal about character is revealed in the hand. I don't want you to become self-conscious and begin looking at your hands now but for me there are various parts of the body that are very significant from the point of view of character: eyes, lips, chin, hands. These to me are all significant features. I'm not talking about the beauty of the features, or the lack of beauty. I am talking of something deeper, something related to character. Hands are very important and I think the hands of Christ would be wonderful hands. They would reveal character, strength, gentleness and love.

The touch of a hand is a very significant thing. There are some people whose hands are quite rough. I don't mean skin-wise, but rough, insensitive. There are other hands that can be strong but they are extremely sensitive. Their touch is gentle, not weak but gentle, and so with the hands of Christ. And, speaking spiritually, if you put on Christ you will develop a very sensitive touch. You will not be ham-fisted, rough, in your approach. You will be gentle— so gentle, so sensitive that Christ will begin to be revealed in and through you.

Whose side are you on in the matter of your hands? Leave them with Satan and self or give them to God—the choice is yours.

Hands, the things that we do. Feet, the places we go. I think you can fill in a good deal of this yourself—Satan's trategy where your feet are concerned.

Again, with a company like this, he is not tending to try to turn your feet to sabbats and black magic circles and all that kind of thing, for generally that has no appeal to people of your type. He settles for areas of wrong-doing that are not extreme—areas which some Christians consider not too bad although others regard them as forbidden.

In my earlier days public cinemas fell into that category, largely I suppose because of the quality of films that tended to be shown. The evangelical world on the whole drew the line and just did not go. Sometimes a very good film was on show but it was often accompanied by one that was less so and the Christian community, not totally, but to a great extent, just cut out cinema going. It wasn't generally approved and the same applied to dance halls and public houses. Opinion was divided but I would guess that the majority of evangelicals viewed those things askance. Some quite bluntly said, 'No, you don't go there,' while others

101

said, 'You should be careful about what you do but it's not a total ban.'

I have never been terribly keen on too rigid a set of rules because sometimes you construct your set of rules and people obey them because they are rules and they resent them, and they never really obey them from the heart. They obey them because they are the commandments of men. Now I would rather have the rules than people doing wrong things but ideally Christ wants to bring souls into a relationship with Himself that causes them to observe His rules because they are written in their hearts and they know them to be the commandment of God and not just the tradition of men.

You may ask, 'Where are you going from there?' Well, I would say there is a golden rule. As you meet the circumstances of life, ask yourself the question, 'What would Jesus do? Is this a place to which Jesus would go?' and if the answer is 'No' you say, 'Well, is it a place to which He would have me go now that He is living in me?' If the sincere answer in your heart is, 'No,' then don't go there. Do not go where you cannot take Christ. I find that a very good rule. In life generally, ask yourself, 'What would Jesus do?' This brings you up sharp because what He would do is so different from what fallen carnal nature would do. Abide by that rule. Do not go where Jesus would not go, or where you would be ashamed to be found were He meeting you in person in that moment. Do not go where He would not go, and do not act as He would not act: just realise that the child of God has Christ within him and he is to do nothing which is dishonouring to Christ—to do nothing that He would not do.

The feet are very important. You'll find, for example, that when a person is following Christ and there sounds the voice of temptation, the person tends to stop and turn to listen. The head is turned in the first instance but not the whole body. Remember Lot's wife—she came out of Sodom but her heart remained in it and she thought about it and she looked back. Now when you look back you normally turn round and it is so with sin and temptation. You hear with the inner ear and you turn to listen and you turn to look and without realising it you have turned right round in the opposite direction. You will find that the way to backsliding is for your feet to turn round, and Satan is after your feet. Are some of you who once walked with God deeply, now facing in a different direction? Have your feet turned round? Oh, you have reasons, many reasons, seemingly good reasons for the courses you have taken but if, in fact, your feet have turned round, you have turned away from God and you are walking in another direction.

Satan wants your feet. He wants you to walk in his ways, and failing to get you on to a way that is deliberately a wrong way, he wants you to walk in a way that is not the way of God—a way that you would judge as being moderate, normal, reasonable—a way that suits—a way that fulfils ordinary human needs. He will settle for that. You do not really want to go back on to the broad road that leads to destruction, but many a soul finds bypaths that lead off the narrow road. They find 'bypath meadow'—a place of unfruitfulness and spiritual death. Beware of the pleasant side road. The way of Life must needs be straight and narrow.

God will not settle for any side road. He wants your feet. God wants to control the places that you go and He is not merely interested in a list of negatives—don't go to the films, don't go to the dance hall, don't go to the pub and so on. We get that kind of thing so deeply into our mind. That's not the kind of thing that God is mainly interested in. He wants feet that are shod with the preparation of the gospel of peace. He wants feet that will run in His service. 'How beautiful upon the mountains are the feet of them that bring good tidings.' He wants runners with the gospel. He wants feet that are active in the affairs of the Kingdom. God never leaves you with only negatives. He always leaves you with positives. To me it is a pathetic thing to think of people sitting in their homes: 'I can't go to the pictures and I'm not allowed to go to the disco and I can't go to the pub—I might as well be dead!' And then they proceed to watch it all on television!

I look back on my own experience and I don't really think you can build life on negatives. If you have nothing but negatives you are in danger of ultimately exploding into rebellion and kicking over the traces. Many a one has said, 'Well I'm jolly well going to the dance halls and I'm going to the discos and I'm going to the pubs. I want to see for myself what it's all about.' I think that can be an understandable human reaction. I haven't found that God deals with me on negatives alone. I have never forgotten the time of my own Baptism in the Holy Spirit. I was working in the country at the time and the ponds were solidly frozen. It had been a particularly hard winter that year and a number of us were thoroughly enjoying skating. I had just managed to teach myself how to skate backwards and I was full of pride in my accomplishment. Skating forwards was fine but skating backwards caused me to feel that I really was somebody! Nobody had taught me. I had picked it up myself and it was wonderful!

Then I was baptised in the Holy Spirit and oh, the wonder and the glory of it! I was absolutely thrilled—thrilled beyond my deepest expectation or anticipation. It was far more glorious, I think, than my fondest dream of it had ever been. I was deeply baptised, gloriously baptised. My whole life was turned upside down. I was touched to deeps that I never knew existed within my being. My Baptism has always been of tremendous significance to me. Do you know, God never said, 'Now look, you are wasting your time skating and you really shouldn't skate. It is a sin to skate!' It isn't a sin to skate. It is a means of progress from one point on the physical plane to another, and I can imagine in some countries it is a very necessary thing. God never said anything about skating being a sin. Quite suddenly I didn't want to skate any more. I had no objection to skating. If I had had to cross a lake somewhere or other I would have been very happy to skate across it, but I was so consumed with the fire of God and the desire to know more of this God that skating seemed a total waste of time. It wasn't getting me anywhere at all except up and down a frozen loch! Now, don't misunderstand, I would encourage youngsters to go skating. If I was in a school situation and there was a frozen loch on which pupils wanted to skate, I would be happy to encourage them. They could skate, or do gymnastics, or play football. These things are all of a kind —all of a piece. There is a time and a place where they are in order but for me there came 'the expulsive power of a greater affection.' It was just as simple as that. Peter and John left their nets and they followed Christ. There was nothing wrong with fishing but it had no more attraction for them in the face of a deeper and more profound call. At the sound of that voice people sometimes leave their jobs and follow Him to the ends of the earth. I have a tremendous respect for some of our missionaries. Having been with two of them for a week or two in South America, I saw and experienced the conditions in which they live. To reach that particular station you travelled for about twelve hours. On the last lap and for much of the journey there was almost no path across desert sand. We travelled in a Land Rover and felt battered in all directions. We arrived absolutely filthy, our clothes full of sand. There were no normal toilet facilities and we slept under mosquito nets. The heat was almost unbearable and the area was suffering from lack of rain. There was a grave food shortage in the village and some people were literally starving, and life was rough.

I remember the late James Salter, one of the founders of Congo (now Zaire) Evangelistic Mission, saying to me once, 'It can be very rough. You can be away from home for years, having left your wife behind. You can be up to your neck almost literally in bog and marsh, dirty, wet and uncomfortable. You know the hard end of life, yet your feet have been taken there by Christ.' Note the words: the feet are taken there by Christ. I found that men of Salter's type were extremely happy. They had faced the cross. They had taken up the cross and they followed the Christ whithersoever He went. I want you to remember that there were the marks of nails in Christ's hands. There was pain in His hands. There were nail prints in His feet and His feet were sore. As men and women of God in our day pick up their crosses they'll have sore feet and sore hands but they'll have Christ. He hasn't promised us easy roads, painless paths, but He has promised to be with us, even to the end of the age. And I would rather walk with Christ with feet suffering agony than walk anywhere with feet at ease without Him.

Again I come to a profound truth that I quote to you often although I'm not sure that you ever really accept it. It is associated with Madame Guyon. She had discovered that wherever she was, on land or sea, in prison or in palace hall, Heaven was there for Christ was there. Wherever she was, Christ was with her, and she was really totally indifferent as to whether she was out at sea in storm, or confined in a prison cell (as she was for years), or being fêted in a palace. She was of the nobility and found all of these conditions in her life—imprisonment, palace luxury, dangers at sea and on land—and she said, 'I have come to a place where I am totally unconcerned because I find that Christ is there wherever I am':

> All scenes alike engaging prove
> To souls imprest with sacred love;
> Where'er they dwell, they dwell in Thee,
> In Heav'n, in earth, or on the sea.

It reminds me of a priest who was imprisoned in South America for his profession of faith in Christ. He was thrown into an awful prison, a solitary cell, filthy. I think it was rat-infested. It was certainly filthy and the stench was awful. The situation was intolerable but Christ came, the light of Christ came, the glory of Christ came and when the hour of release arrived the man was extremely reluctant to come out, for Christ was there.

I heard a part of a testimony recently that reminded me of a biography[1] that some of you have read. A man was imprisoned in extremely cold, icy, intolerable conditions and suddenly down from the ceiling there came a warm draught of air although there was neither ventilator nor opening above. Supernatural intervention—the hand of God.

He will never allow your hands to be so sore that you can't go on working even although there are nails driven through them. He will never allow your feet to be so pierced and torn that you can't go on walking in His way. As for me, I want Christ to have my feet. You may give yours to the devil if you wish but know that they will both pay wages, both Christ and the devil. God grant that you make the right choice. Of one thing I can assure you: if you walk the devil's way there is no point in expecting wages at Heaven's door. You will receive the wages from the one whom you serve, the one in whose ways you walk.

So, shall we just for a moment review the ground we have covered? Who will have the mind? Who will control eye-gate and ear-gate? Who will have control of the tongue?

Will we choose a stiff neck or a neck under the yoke—a neck and shoulders under the yoke of God? Who will have the heart? To whom will the knees bow? For whom will the hands work? In whose service will the feet run? Will you be lost through an Achilles heel? Will you end up with a backbone or not? God grant that we will all allow Him to occupy all the vital areas of our bodies that our weak points may become strongholds in His hands.

Note

[1] Myrna Grant, *Vanya* (Kingsway, 1974).

7

A Delicate Matter

When the idea of including a chapter on the organs of reproduction first occurred to me, I rejected it as being much too sensitive for a book of even this kind. The subject was not preached on in the series of sermons on which the book is based, but the idea would not go away. People of my generation are generally reluctant to speak of intimate matters in public—or indeed in private for that matter— but surely a stage has been reached in our society when certain of our inhibitions will have to be cast off and straight and frank speaking employed. Perhaps some of us have been too silent for too long while others, of different views, have proclaimed their polluted thoughts all across the land —through radio, T.V. and the media generally.

I am aware, of course, that some aspects of the subject have been dealt with in earlier chapters—particularly in relation to the eyes and the ears, but I would like to add a few more direct comments before bringing this section of the book to a close.

What is God's attitude to sex? Let me state it plainly. God created us male and female and the woman was created to be a helpmeet for man. The man needed her and she needed him. Marriage was instituted by God and had His blessing as is clear through the Old and New Testaments. In Genesis God said, 'Therefore shall a man leave his father and his mother, and shall cleave unto his wife; and they shall be one flesh.' Christ repeated this, and He Himself honoured marriage with His own presence at Cana in Galilee. The writer of Hebrews states plainly that 'marriage is honourable in all, and the bed undefiled.' Paul also indicated clearly that sex met a human need as well as having a procreational purpose (see 1 Cor 7:5). There is no doubt about the Divine sanction for marriage. There is equally no doubt about Divine disapproval of sex outwith marriage. It is completely and consistently frowned upon throughout the whole Bible. No compromise over thousands of years is even hinted at to suit changing fashions and customs. It is forbidden.

When all the teaching of the New Testament is taken into account the following position emerges. For followers of Christ two ways open:

a) *The way of marriage*. But a believer may enter this relationship only with a fellow believer. There is to be no unequal yoking with an unbeliever. Marriage is to be a permanent relationship; divorce is not the will of God but may be allowed for sexual unfaithfulness. Where a marriage is broken through desertion by one partner, the person deserting is not allowed to remarry while the other remains alive.

b) *The way of celibacy*. Christ clearly said, 'For there are eunuchs, which were so born from their mother's womb: and there are eunuchs, which were made eunuchs by men: and there are eunuchs, which made themselves eunuchs for the kingdom of heaven's sake.' Paul speaks highly of this state for those who share his own gift of continency. The consequence of these teachings is that some have regarded the celibate state as a superior state to that of marriage and some have come into bondage on the matter. Now there is no doubt that in Heaven there will be no marriage and we will all be tuned for life on that plane, but on earth we must face the reality of the situation that exists. For some people the way to the highest is through marriage; for others it is through bypassing marriage. Let every one be led of God.

In either case, those parts of the body which are involved are to be kept in holiness. When there is control there is force conserved which can be used for God. Too often people think negatively on this subject—that if there is sexual misbehaviour there will be a loss of spiritual power, and forget that there is also a positive side—if there is sexual control there will be positive power. Many a zealous follower of Christ has found that through this discipline he or she has greatly deepened in the life of God—indeed has been almost propelled on to higher planes. God is interested in the area positively and not merely to guard it from evil. I want you to understand the positive aspect clearly. It is very important. Use your sexual instincts as a means of progress but do not come into bondages that God does not bring. Be controlled of God. either within honourable marriage or in a celibate state. Aim for the highest and let God take you His way to that goal.

There is perhaps one warning note I should sound to young people. It is very natural to desire marriage and to immerse yourself in another's life. If you do this before your heart's deep allegiance is given to Christ it can be very difficult thereafter to retract the position, and then give Christ first place. Always remember He demands this. You will find it much easier to have your relationship with Him established before you let your love flow freely to another. Put Christ first and let Him lead. If your partner is God's choice for you, you will find that you can give an overflow of love which in the end will be far deeper than would have been the case had you chosen a direct relationship with the other from which Christ was excluded or because of which

111

He was relegated to second place. God's way is perfect—but always has in it elements of discipline and sacrifice. When these are accepted, the glory that ensues will seem to you to be incalculably greater than what you felt you might lose.[1]

There is another side—the dark side. As God is interested in preserving your purity, purity which is so closely linked with power—so Satan is determined to destroy it. Perhaps there is no area in the lives of men that is more viciously attacked. We have noticed in earlier chapters of this book how he attacks through ear-gate and eye-gate and attempts to fill the mind with unclean thoughts. He has his hand on much of the media and pumps his filth into our very homes. Sexual deviation ruins lives. Individuals go down through immorality. Nations perish, as for example ancient Rome. When vice and sexual corruption get a grip on a nation retribution always seems to follow.

So, young believer, be on your guard. Lives are made or broken on this issue. You will never be greatly used of God and be unclean. Attend to purity and leave God to attend to power. The two are forever linked. You may say, and so many do say, as they come for help, 'I have tried but I fall again and again. I don't know what to do to get victory. I come into a meeting and am convicted. I resolve not to fall again, but temptation comes on me and in spite of myself I fall, and it happens again and again. What can I do? I am at the end of my tether.' Well, first, that is an excellent place to be—at the end of your tether. It is here that God so often intervenes in lives—when you know you are beaten. While you still think you can overcome in your own strength you are likely to fail. When you are forced into dependency on His strength you are on the way to victory.

One of the problems that many a sincere person meets on this front results from ignorance, and ignorance can form a basis on which Satan brings false condemnation when there is no real guilt. Let me explain. If you had been dabbling in the occult and become involved in the dark arts and had come to me for advice I would tell you to renounce these things completely and never to turn to them again. I would expect them to die. But if you come to me about sexual difficulty I can't say, 'Sex is wrong—turn from it entirely. Repress your every sexual instinct and desire.' As well as it being impossible for you to do this it would also be wrong. What I must do is let you know clearly that it is not sinful to have sexual desires—that it is perfectly natural. Sin, you must realise, does not lie in having desire, it lies in how desire is handled. Sex can have a God-given outlet through marriage or sublimation[2]. If it is allowed to control you, rather than being controlled, it can wreck not only your whole lifework for God but your very life as well. 'Every sin,' God says, 'that a man doeth is without his body; but he that committeth fornication sinneth against his own body.' The body of a Christian is a temple of the Holy Spirit and is to be kept in sanctification—'If any man destroyeth the temple of God, him shall God destroy' (1 Cor 3:17).

Preachers often evade this but I feel I should be blunt. The words I quote are the words of God. Paul wrote:

Wherefore God gave them up in the lusts of their hearts unto uncleanness, that their bodies should be dishonoured among themselves.... For this cause God gave them up unto vile passions: for their women changed the natural use into that which is against nature: and likewise also the men, leaving the natural use of the woman, burned in their lust one toward another, men with men working unseemliness, and receiving in themselves that recompense of their error which was due (Rom 1:24,26–27).

This totally condemns homosexuality and lesbianism. While we may have great sympathy for people who suffer from this, particularly for those who have been born this way rather than having acquired the taste, we may not condone the practices. The fact that a number of church leaders have pronounced on the other side, in no way alters the clear teaching of the Bible. We must declare unequivocally against what God regards as sin.

This leads me to my closing points. Elsewhere I have referred to the difficulty most people have in understanding gross sin. Normal temptation and wrong-doing, yes; but gross immorality, bestiality, violent sex, muggings, etc., lie outwith the understanding of most normal people.

It seems to me that as there is a progression in holiness so is there in evil. We pass upward in our life with God from stage to stage. If we secure ground we are challenged to take more ground—so in lives which go downward. If a soul loses ground there comes new temptation and further falls. Old partial satisfaction palls and new areas of sin appeal. These in turn fail to satisfy and lure on to yet deeper depths of depravity. Souls don't reach the lowest depths suddenly but in gradual stages. That which at one time would have been utterly repulsive becomes attractive, until evil has separated the individual even from ordinary fallen fellow men. The pilgrim's progress has a counterpart in the dupe's regress. You will have noticed that on the progress side development is from stage to stage. All is not attained in a moment. Deep holiness does not come full blown overnight. As there is regression downwards so there is progression upwards.

Watch the body generally and this most delicate part of it particularly. It can become a highway to deep Heaven (as C. S. Lewis might have said) or to the depths of unutterable hell.

Notes

[1] Counsellors should also take into account that the economics of modern life often make marriage impossible for young people long after nature has been driving along this line.

[2] I have been asked to expand a little on what I mean by sublimation. Sometimes enquirers are given advice which leads to repression. Sin is identified and the enquirer advised to resist it. Desires are denied expression and forced down into the subconscious. There they fester and in due time explode—frequently into deep sin. Sometimes they surface in sleeping experiences. Surely there is a better way. Instead of a person trying to persuade himself that a desire is wrong, has been put away and is dead, etc., he would be better to say, 'Oh God, I have this unholy desire. I acknowledge it.' He can let it surface before God and feel it pass away in the light of God's presence. He suddenly feels whole and free from obsession. He is now in a position to let his energies and love go out and up to God and become dedicated to His service. Instead of being repressed, desire has been sublimated and redirected. The world owes a great debt to countless men and women of God who have found and walked this way. (This definition of sublimation is not quite the same as that of professional psychologists!)

PART 2

THE TESTIMONY OF THE REV JOHN HAMILTON

8

Author's Introduction

To many of my readers John Hamilton will need no introduction. I am reminded of an occasion when I introduced
Jackie Pullinger to 1,800 people. I am sure many in that
audience knew of Jackie Pullinger but wondered who on
earth I was! I have known Johnnie over many years. When I
first met him he was in what I might describe as a Pentecostal
'wilderness'—confused, somewhat disillusioned—but
hungry. By God's grace he found the way again. I remember
it so clearly. He heard me preach on Pentecost and revival
and the relationship between the two and invited me to his
church—and then took cold feet. I think that this was the
only occasion in my life in which I put any pressure on a
person to allow me to fulfil an engagement—but I knew I
had to go. God met us wonderfully. John came back into
full Pentecostal blessing. His wife, Zillah, was baptised.
Many were mightily filled with the Spirit and a relationship
began with Mr and Mrs Hamilton and many of their people
which has continued through the years.

In more recent days I have been delighted at the power of
Mr Hamilton's ministry and at the operation of the gift of
knowledge through him. In one of our gatherings of perhaps

400–500 people he spoke of various conditions that God had revealed to him and then particularly indicated the prevalence of fear in many lives—fear to witness for Christ. When he asked those concerned to stand I was amazed. About 50–60 rose. I knew many of those people and I had never suspected the bondage of fear in their lives. (I had forgotten that in my own early days God had set me free of a fear which I had never known was there until He took it away.) One of the people dealt with that night had a remarkable experience. As she rose to her feet she felt something drop off her. I had always regarded her as a very forceful and confident young lady. But the truth was otherwise. She was held back by fear. It dropped off and God spoke to her. He asked her if she was willing to obey Him totally—to give up everything for Him. She considered the matter and concluded she had nothing much left in life but God, and she might as well go the whole way. She had nothing to lose. God then gave her what I felt were very strange instructions and she went ahead with a project which brings a whole group of unsaved people under the gospel every week. It has been remarkably successful.

Back to Johnnie Hamilton. His ministry bears rich fruit. It is compassionate and discerning. Unknown numbers are being set free as Christ flows through him. In *Reflections on the Gifts of the Spirit* I have already written of some aspects of the revelation ministry in which he is used and of the compassion of Christ that moves him.

Read now his own story in his own words, as adapted from taped addresses.

9

Early Days

I don't think I will ever, ever forget the first time I gave a testimony. It wasn't in a place like this[1]—it was a very small mission hall with about forty people present. I was only maybe a month or so converted, and a young man from Edinburgh had taken me to a little place called Elphinstone, to a Faith Mission Conference. It was all new to me, everything was new. The conference was the kind where there were two speakers. After the first speaker had given his word, there was a break for tea and then the second speaker came on. I'll never forget that day. On the platform there was a table nicely spread with lovely crockery and nice cakestand and everything just so nice: and that was for the platform party. But it was different for poor people sitting in the stalls. When it came to tea-time, I saw two ladies come out of the kitchen with the biggest kettles I ever saw in all my life. One had a big zinc basin full of cracked cups, which she handed out; behind her came another lady with bags of buns, and that was your afternoon tea. The lady with this great big kettle reached me: *'With or without?'* Well, it wouldn't have made any difference, because it was stewed to glory!

Anyway, the time came when the young man who had brought me went up to the platform and spoke to the leader and said,

'There's a young fellow here, he's not been long saved; would you like to hear his testimony?'

And of course they said, 'Yes, get him up'—fresh blood —I suspect they hadn't had a new testimony for many years. I had no notion of what was going on even when my young friend stood on the platform after tea was over and the second speaker was ready to come on, and said,

'Well, friends, you'll be glad to know I've brought my young brother with me this afternoon.'

I thought, 'I can't remember seeing your young brother.'

And he said, 'He's only been saved for a few months.'

And I thought, 'That is marvellous.'

And he said, 'He used to be a barman.'

I thought, 'That is unbelievable!'

And he said, 'Would you like to hear his testimony?'

I always sit at the front, and I'm sitting, saying, 'Yes, I would like to hear his testimony!' And I thought, 'I'll listen to what *he* says, and if ever I'm asked to give *my* testimony, I'll just say what he says, because we're in the same boat.'

Nobody moved. And I thought, 'What is keeping his brother? He's either an old age pensioner, or he's crippled —there's something wrong with him.'

Now my mother always said, 'Never look back: it's bad manners.' And you know, even at twenty-five, I still kept that rule—I never looked back. But I was tempted; I thought, 'Who is this brother?' And then he said to me, 'It's you, brother.' And I said, '*Me?*'... And I remember there were three steps up to the platform; I fell up the first two, and on the third one I grabbed the tablecover. Have you ever given your testimony standing on sugar? It'll be the sweetest testimony you're ever likely to give! The whole place was chaos. And after all the chaos and all that great big build-up, all I said was, 'Well, friends, I'm glad I'm saved.' And I sat down again. Needless to say, I was never asked back there again.

Anyway, when I got outside I said to this young fellow, 'Don't you go round telling everybody you're my brother!' But he said, 'You are my brother.'

I said, 'Look, I've only got two, and you're not one of them.'

And it was then he started to tell me of this great family of God. Isn't this a wonderful family to belong to? And it's only through the blood of Jesus, only through that saving knowledge of Christ, that I can say to you tonight, I'm so glad that I belong to the family of God. I've got so many brothers and sisters it's unbelievable, and I'm glad that I belong to that family. I want to tell you tonight how I came into the family.

Let me take you back almost sixty years, to a wee place in Coatbridge where I was born. There were six of us: boy, girl, boy, girl, boy, girl—how's that for an order? I thought my home was ordinary, but maybe you will think it was extraordinary. My mother was a Roman Catholic, and my father was a Protestant. And every Sunday there were arguments in our home. I mean, there were arguments through the week, but Sunday was extra-special. There was a regular pattern: my mother would say, 'They're going to the Catholic church,' and my father would say, 'Oh no, they're going to the Protestant church.'

Catholic church, Protestant church—you know what happened? We were sent to both. How about that for punishment? Every Sunday we had four services, and through the week we had four services, and my mother and father said, 'And you'll go there until you're sixteen.' Now if there are any mathematicians here, you just count that up. Sunday was the blackest day of my life. I just did not enjoy Sunday, going through all the services. I think the only Sunday I enjoyed was when we had the Sunday School Prize-giving Service. The whole Hamilton family got Bibles for perfect attendance at church. Not perfect behaviour—perfect attendance. And every year the minister said, 'John Hamilton, for perfect attendance at church, a lovely copy of the Word of God.' And I would say under my breath, 'Aw, not another Bible'—because for good attendance you got a book, but for perfect attendance you got a Bible; and every year I knew I'd get a Bible. And every year my mother would say, 'Let me see your Bibles...right, put them in the cupboard.' She never even said, 'Read them,' just, 'Put them in the cupboard.' If Underground Evangelism had known about the Hamiltons, they could have had a cupboardful of Bibles!

But anyhow, this Sunday Toshie McGrory was sitting next to me. And he said (and I couldn't believe what I was hearing), 'I wish I could get a Bible.'

I thought, 'This guy's bananas.' I said: 'What, you really want a Bible?' 'Aye,' he said, 'but I'll no' get one.' I said, 'I've got news for you.' He said, 'What's that?' I said, 'You can have mine, on one condition: you give me your book.' And right under the minister's nose I was arranging to swop the Bible for a book. And sure enough, my name was called out, I got the Bible and came back to my seat. And I thought Toshie McGrory's name would never get called out. But you know what the minister said?

'Toshie McGrory, for good attendance at church, *The Dandy Annual*.'

What! I nearly jumped out of the seat, I was so excited.

'What! *The Dandy Annual!* You bring that *Dandy Annual* on Monday, I'll bring the Bible to school—okay?' And right enough, when I got home:

'Let me see your Bibles...right, put them in the cupboard'—the usual.

Next morning I took the Bible out of the cupboard,

shoved it up my jersey, ran to school (first time I ever ran to school), and there was Toshie with the book at the gate. I don't know anything the teacher told us that morning because I was under the desk with Keyhole Kate and Desperate Dan—I had a great time.

But then, when I got home, my mother and my father's sister, my Auntie Mary (who was in the Christian Brethren), were having afternoon tea. And my mother, just to impress my Christian Brethren auntie, said, 'Let your Auntie Mary see that lovely Bible you got yesterday!' And I don't know if it was a brainwave or a brainstorm, but I thought, 'I'll just give her last year's—she'll never know the difference. They're all the same.' So I took last year's Bible and I gave it to her. And everything was going my way until she put her glasses on. And she looked at the front cover—'Oh,' she said, 'they've made a mistake.' And by this time I was halfway out the door. My mother said, 'What mistake have they made?' She said, 'They've put down *last year* and not *this year*.' My mother said, '*That* is no mistake! What did you do with that Bible you got yesterday at church?' And when I told her in front of my Brethren Auntie Mary that I swopped the Bible for *The Dandy Annual*..! I've got the mark here—she just thumped me, right there and then.

Now, I'm only telling you that to tell you this. Every Sunday four services; every year a Bible for perfect attendance; and yet I didn't know why Jesus came. I had no idea. The only God I knew was an angry God, a God Who judged people, a God Who was always ready to condemn them. I never once heard of the love of God. I never once knew that Jesus came to die for my sins. Now I don't blame the church for that in this sense, because when the minister stood up—and here's another thing I couldn't understand —he never once changed his introduction all the years I went there. He said the usual phrase every Sunday morning, and when he said it I switched off: 'My text for today is...'

And that's when I switched off. Now you can switch off—and I can tell the ones who switch off; I'm an expert. I switched off every Sunday. I looked as though I was listening, but I was miles away. I filled in the time while he was preaching by looking down from the balcony and counting all the ladies who wore hats. And if he was still preaching, I would count all the men with bald heads. I would do anything rather than listen to the Word. So I can't blame the preacher, because I didn't *listen* to the Word. But I just know this: that I did not want to keep going to church every Sunday. And I knew I would be there until I was sixteen.

Note

[1] City Hall, Glasgow.

10

Behind the Bar

But, you know, I didn't wait till I was sixteen. Before I was sixteen I ran away from home. I came from Coatbridge to Edinburgh, and when I got there I discovered two things. One, I didn't have a job; two, I had nowhere to sleep. And that was a bad start. But I got a newspaper, and down the 'Situations Vacant' column was a job for me. Are you listening?

'Smart young man.' Everybody laughs when I tell them that. 'Smart young man, must have good appearance.' But that wasn't what caught my attention. What really caught my attention were other three words: 'Must live in.' The job that was being advertised was for a trainee barman in the biggest hotel in Edinburgh, which is the North British. And so I went for my interview, and standing there in the cocktail bar the manager asked me many questions, and I told him many lies, just to get the job. Then he said, 'Stand up.' 'I am standing.' 'You're what!! Laddie, you're too wee—you'll never reach the beer pumps! Away you go and try them.' And I went over to the bar and I tried to reach these beer pumps, and I couldn't—I just couldn't get them. He said, 'I'm sorry, son, you're no good to me if you can't reach the beer pumps.' I was so disappointed. I didn't want to be a barman. But I wanted that room. That's all I wanted—not the job, the room.

However, as I walked out, I saw an empty beer box in the corner, and I said to him, 'Excuse me.' 'What is it?' 'If I had that empty beer box over at the beer pumps, I could reach them then.'

He said, 'Right, my boy, the job's yours.' And I was christened in a cocktail bar 'Half-Pint Hamilton' (how about that for a name?). And I got the room. And when I walked into this room, I couldn't believe it: there was only one bed, and only one barman—that was me—in that bed. Because —I was brought up with six in one bed: three at he top and three at the bottom. And I thought, 'Boy, this is really living! One bed for me!' And I went down the next day to go through the barman's training.

And when the door opened and the customers came in, I couldn't believe it. Now I don't know about you; but I used to think that people who went to church were the ones who were going to Heaven, and they were miserable—hello?— and the people who went to pubs, they were going to hell, and they were happy—hello? isn't that right? You're not too sure about that one. Well, that's what I was brought up to believe. People who went to pubs were going to hell. But they were happy. And I remember saying, standing in that bar that day, 'I don't want to go to hell. But I want to be happy. So I'll join this lot.' Now God gives us a free will, isn't that right? And I decided that day that God and the Church and Christians were not for me. These were my people. And I was going to have a great time. I would do what they did, I would live as they lived, and I would have that happy look that they had—because that's what I was after: I was after happiness. I wanted to be happy, because all my childhood I had been unhappy. I won't tell you the full story, but I had a very, very unhappy childhood. I was always the weak one of the family. Being the smallest didn't help either. But I was always sickly, I was always the poorest, and I was always unhappy. And so when I ran away from home, I felt I wasn't losing anything. I just wanted the door to close, and I would do my own thing. I would be my own boss, I would live my life, and I would enjoy it. I wasn't even sixteen, just fifteen and a half. And I determined that I would never again go into a church, or mix amongst Christians. And I started living as these people lived; I started doing what they did.

And I'm going to tell you something: *I was so happy doing it that I tried suicide three times.*

I didn't talk about it; I tried it. That's how happy I was. It's a lie, it's a lie. That look of happiness is a mask; and that mask is on many a face. It's a mask that says 'Ha, ha, ha,' and inside people are crying. Inside they are really crying. Inside they're broken in so many pieces that they'll never come together. But I've got news for you: they can come together tonight by the touch of Jesus. He knows man's every need. He knows where we are, and He knows how we are, and He wants us to know that purpose: that Jesus is the answer to our every need.

I was so unhappy, and I was so lonely, do you know I was so full of fear, I was so depressed, I went to one psychiatrist after another. I knew I wasn't crazy; I just knew there was something I needed to know but nobody seemed to come up with the answers. I went from one thing to another; I tried spiritism, I tried all sorts of things, but everything I tried just left me more frustrated. And do you know, I got to the place where I thought, 'What is the use? What is the use of going on? There is nothing to go on for.' I wasn't even twenty-five, and already three times I'd tried suicide. I said I was depressive, I was full of fear, I was never alone but I always felt lonely, full of insecurity. But you would never ever have guessed I had all these problems. Do you know why? I lived a lie. I would have got the Academy award for being the best actor of the year. I had a face for the public, and that face, I tell you, deceived many many people. You could hear me laughing the loudest, you could hear me swearing the loudest, you could hear me joking the loudest. But inside, I wept and I wept and I wept. I can't remember a night that I didn't weep before I fell asleep. But never once did I call on God. Never once did I go to church. Never once did I look for a Christian. And to tell you straight—the reason simply was this, that when I went to church, I never once saw a happy face. When I sat in that church, it seemed so unreal; the people did not seem real. It was like walking into a graveyard; there was a deadness about the whole thing. Be careful with young people, they are very, very impressionable. I looked round that congregation almost every Sunday, looking, searching for even a kind face, and I never saw one, never saw one. I listened for someone with a friendly voice and never heard one. The only time people spoke to me was when I misbehaved: '*Shh!*' Boy, I've got digs on my ribs from my brother and my sister at either side: '*You're in church, behave!*' And so, I want you to understand that even in my darkest moments, even at times when I wanted so much to have somebody help me, I never thought on God. The only God I knew, as I told you, was an angry God, a God Who was away up there, and just ready to strike me if I walked out of place.

11

The Dawn of Hope

But on the twenty-eighth of August, down on Portobello
Beach, I was walking along the Prom. I will never forget it.
Gathered there must have been two to three hundred people
on the sands. And they were singing:

> Blessed assurance, Jesus is mine!

*   *   *   *   *

> This is my story, this is my song,
>   Praising my Saviour all the day long.

I never saw such happy people! I thought, 'They can't be
Christians—they're too happy.' And I thought, 'Maybe it's
an American group that's come over, and it's a new religion
that's come to Scotland!' That's right: that's what I thought.
And on the makeshift platform was a sign: Faith Mission
Campaign. And on that platform were five young men. And
I tell you, folks, their faces were radiant. Do you ever speak
to yourself? Do you? I remember saying to myself: 'Look at
them! They don't smoke, they don't drink, they don't

gamble, they don't go to the dancing, they don't don't don't and they are happy! Look at you. You do all these things and you are miserable.' And that was a true assessment of my life. I was twenty-five, I had a drink problem, depression—I tell you, my life was just in one mess, and I was standing there, looking down on these five young men, and there was just something about these young men that arrested me. They were so fulfilled, they were so clean, they were so wholesome. I was the very opposite.

And I thought, 'When they start preaching, I'm off. I've heard it all before.' And I thought the speaker would stand up as my old minister did every Sunday and say, 'My text for tonight is....' Boy, was I in for a shock! This guy got me completely off guard. This is what he said: the moment they stopped singing, he stood there and he said,

'I believe God is speaking to someone here tonight.'

Phew! That just blew my mind. He said it again, but this time he pointed right across the Prom. And I remember that finger: it looked like six feet long. He said, 'I believe God is speaking to someone here tonight. Is it you?' And I almost shouted, 'Yes, of course it's me, get on with it.'

But he didn't wait for the answer. I want you to hear what he said:

'If it's you, I want you to know *Jesus loves you.*'

Three words. But they were anointed by the Holy Ghost. They went right into my heart. *Jesus loves you.* Simple words. And I had sung it many times as a wee boy in Sunday School: 'Jesus loves me, this I know.' But that night, something happened. That night, I just knew, these were not just three words, these were eternal truths: *Jesus loves you.*

And for the first time, I began to cry in public. Oh, I had cried many times behind a closed door, but never in public —and trust me to do it in front of three hundred people: what a way to start! And I could not stop those tears; they just flowed down my face. As I stood there I said to myself, 'You know what you need? You need Jesus. You need Jesus.' I tell you, that was a revelation to me.

I had no sooner said it, than one of these Faith Mission lads was standing right beside me, and he said, 'Excuse me, sir—.' Of course the mask came on again; I said, 'Get lost.'

'Oh no,' he said, 'You're the one that's lost.' Wasn't that a classic answer? 'You're the one that's lost. And Jesus came to seek and to save the lost.'

And there was something about this young man that really bugged me. I wanted rid of him; I just wanted his back—because there was such a challenge there. And I didn't like it, I was afraid of it—there was just something about this young man: he spoke about *Jesus* and about *God* personally—not vague and general—he spoke about Jesus as if Jesus was standing right there by his side. And it frightened me. We need men like that today. We need such testimonies. It really frightened me. And I wanted rid of this man. And so I started saying, 'Look, I don't believe in all this.' And I thought, 'The best way to get rid of him is to pour a lot of filth on to him, and he'll start running. He'll not stop till he gets to church.'

But how wrong I was! The more filth I poured on that young fellow, the more he just stood there and said, 'John, that's not what it's all about. Jesus loves you.'

I thought, 'If he says that again, I'll thump him.' Because every time he said it I felt a lump in my throat. And then he said to me, 'Would you like to come tomorrow night, to the closing meeting in the Baptist Church?'

I thought, 'Here's my chance: now I'll get rid of him. If I say, 'No, I can't come,' he'll stand there, but if I say, 'Yes I'd love to come,' he'll go away thinking he's done a good night's work and I'll be rid of him.' I said, 'I'd love to come.'

Now, humanly speaking I couldn't be there because I

had only two nights free, and that was a Sunday night and a Friday night. This was a Sunday night, and he was asking me to come to a Monday night meeting. I felt so safe, I said, 'Yes, I would love to come. What time does it start? Who's the speaker?' Oh, so clever! He held out a card and he looked me right in the face: 'Are you sure you'll come?' I said, 'Look, if I say I'll be there, I'll be there. Give me your card.' And he held that card. And he looked at me eyeball to eyeball and said, 'God bless you. We'll be praying for you.' And that did it. Nobody had ever said that to me. Nobody had ever cared. But that young fellow, a total stranger: 'God bless you! We'll be praying for you.' We need Christians like that.

And I found out six months later that from that night those five young men—thank God for them—prayed the whole night through for my salvation. How about that, Christians? The whole night through they prayed that I would get saved. No wonder I couldn't sleep that night. Could you have slept, five men praying for you all night? And all through the night I kept hearing, 'God is speaking to you. You need Jesus. Jesus loves you,' and so on. And I thought, 'I wish it was morning. These Bible punchers, they've got me at a sentimental time. I'll be all right in the morning—I'll be back to my old miserable self in the morning.' Imagine wanting to get back to your old miserable self again!

Do you believe that God hears prayer? Do you believe He answers prayer? Do you? I believe it. The very next morning, the manager said to me, 'I want to speak to you.'

'What is it?'

'I want you to change your half-day.'

I thought these Faith Mission lads had phoned up and said, 'Give that wee barman a half-day today!'

'Eh, when—when do you want me to change it to?'

'Today.' I said to myself, 'Any day but Monday,' and to

him, 'But why Monday?'

'Well, Vera, the barmaid, has a wedding on Friday. She's asked me to ask you if you'll change.'

And folks, I heard myself saying, 'I'll change.' Now the minute I said that, I realised that I was now free to go to the closing meeting of this seaside campaign. I had no intentions, but remember, five men had prayed.

And I went to the dancing instead. And right there, dancing with this beautiful girl on the dance floor, an irresistible desire to get to the Baptist Church was so strong that I said to this girl, 'Excuse me, darlin', I've got a date somewhere else.' And I walked away and I left her right on her tod! I'll not tell you what she said—she was no lady ...boy!

Now the Baptist Church in Portobello is the hardest church to find. It's not a normal church building, but an upstairs hall. I looked for the Baptists and I couldn't find them. I found every church but the Baptists, and every church was locked. Some were even padlocked. And in that moment I was angry. An anger rose up within me: 'H'm, that's just like the church! Every church is closed, and every pub is open! I'll forget all about this religion; I'll just go and have a drink.'

I looked at my watch; my watch had stopped. I looked up at the town clock. But it wasn't the clock that got my attention. It was underneath the clock: it said, 'Baptist Church.' Isn't that wonderful? You might call it coincidence; I call it God-incidence. I call it God answering prayer. I looked both ways; I wasn't practising kerb drill—I was just making sure none of my mates saw me going into a church on a Monday night. And I was one hour late! How about that for your first time back?

I went up the stairs, and I opened the door, and the man at the door looked at me, and he said, 'I think you've come to the wrong place.' 'Is this not the Baptist Church?' 'Yes.'

'Well, I've come to the right place.' And he looked at me again—no, the second time he X-rayed me: he just examined me from head to toe. (You see, then I was a teddy-boy.)

But one of the young men on the platform who prayed the whole night through for me—the young man that spoke to me—said, 'Oh, John Hamilton!' And everybody looked round, to see who John Hamilton was. I think they thought the Bishop had arrived! and here's this five-feet-nothing. He said, 'Come away.' Now do you remember the teddy-boy style—the jacket with the false shoulders? You go out like that and you come in like this, and the haircut and the tie—the lace for a tie—and the great big crepe-soled shoes —I wish they'd bring those back again—about three or four inches. He said, 'Come away.' And there was only one seat empty: guess where it was...right at the front. He said, 'Come away.' And the only thing that broke the silence down that aisle was these shoes: *squeak, squeak, squeak, squeak*. And I sat right in the front. And he stopped preaching and he gave his testimony.

And everything that young fellow said was my life in duplicate. And there came a cry in my heart that night, 'If only I knew God like he knows Him! If only I had this peace and this joy! If only—if only—if only...' And he said, 'Maybe you're sitting there tonight and you're saying, if only you were like me, if only you had this peace, if only you had this joy....' He said, 'Tonight you can have it.'

Folks, I nearly fell off my seat: I couldn't believe it. He said, 'We're going to bow our heads, we're going to close our eyes. I'm going to ask you tonight if you want Jesus Christ to come into your life and be your Saviour—if you just raise your hand I will see it, I will pray for you, and you'll be born again.' And I said in my heart, 'That's what I'll do—I'll raise my hand....'

Do you know, folks, I could not—I wanted to, but I could not raise it. I knew nothing about the powers of darkness, in that sense; I knew nothing about spiritual warfare; but I believe tonight as I tell you that hell itself was fighting for my soul—I believe that. But remember, five men had prayed—isn't that wonderful?—five men had prayed. And I tried to raise my hand, and I couldn't raise it.

He said, 'Perhaps you couldn't raise your hand? If you just look up, I'll see you, and I'll pray for you.' I tried to look up, and again I could not lift my head. It was as if another hand was holding it down: I could not raise it.

And this young fellow said, 'Perhaps you couldn't raise your hand? perhaps you couldn't even look up? But if you'll just come and see me after the service, I'll have a word of prayer with you. I'll point you to Scriptures that will make you wise to salvation. You'll leave this church tonight knowing your sins are forgiven and you are a child of God.'

And I remember in my heart saying, 'Yes, that's what I'll do. I'll see this Bible-puncher afterwards, and I'll pray, and I'll go out here a child of God.' That's what I wanted to do. We sang a hymn, we closed with the benediction; the meeting was over. I got up out of my seat, and I ran—not to the front: I ran out the door.

But guess what? *He got up*—and he ran after me! And he was a better runner than me! And he said, 'Stop! you're not leaving here until you get right with God.' Oh, I tell you, folks, we need, we need such men today. Jesus said, 'I will make you fishers of men'—isn't that right? 'Stop, you're not leaving here until you get right with God.'

I said, 'Look, I'm sorry for the way I spoke to you last night'—and I meant it. He said, 'Forget last night'—he wasn't standing there licking his wounds like some Christians I know. He said, 'We're speaking about now. God is speaking to you now, John.'

I said, 'Look, I could never *be* a Christian.' He said, 'Why?' I said, 'I am such a sinner, you don't know the people I run around with. I'm just no good—I never have

been any good—I never will be any good. I'm just a sinner.'
And I painted myself as black as I could, thinking he'd say,
'Jesus is wonderful—but He's not that wonderful.'

And he said, 'You're the very one that Jesus came for. He
didn't come for the righteous; He came for sinners.'

I said, 'But look, I could never keep it up. Even if I did
try, I could never keep it up. I'm the weakest of the weak: I
know what I'm like. And I wouldn't like to make a fool of
this; I don't want to do this and then find two days later, or
even two hours later, I'm back to the old John Hamilton
again.'

He said, 'John, I tell you this. If you give your life to
Jesus Christ, He'll not only save you, He'll keep you. You
will be kept by the power of God. There's no man can argue
against that.'

But I said, 'Look, just leave me.' Again that fear came
in—that feeling of fear came in again. There was something
about this young man that really—it was as if God spoke to
me, not a man. I was afraid of it. I said, 'Look, just leave
me.'

He was very wise. If you pray all night for somebody,
God will give you wisdom. God will give you the right words
to speak. God will show you when to be still, and when to go
on, when to speak and when to be silent. You try it. Try the
whole night praying for one man, and you'll not make a
mess of it the next day. He was very wise. That's where he
stopped. And I know tonight that if he'd pushed me just at
that moment, I would not be here. I know that. And this is
what he said:

'All right, John, I'll leave you in the hands of God.' What
does the Bible say? 'It is a fearful thing to fall into the hands
of the Living God.'

He went to the bookstall and got a book, and said, 'I'd
like you to read this book.'

'Oh,' I said, 'how much is it?'

He said, 'I'm giving it to you.'

Now, folks, that really touched me. A total stranger was giving me this book, and all he asked me to do was read it.

12

Free at Last

It was a book of testimonies.

You see how wise the young man was? A book of testimonies. I think there were twenty-five testimonies from people of all different walks in life: they all came to the Cross, they all came to a point of decision for Jesus Christ. And I went home that night, and I read that book from cover to cover, and I wept my way through it. At two o'clock in the morning I got down on my knees. And I wasn't caring—I wasn't caring what anybody thought now or what anybody said, or what anybody would do. I just knew that at that moment I was going to give my life to Jesus Christ.

And when I got down on my knees, I discovered a terrible truth. I didn't know how to pray—I just didn't know how to pray. You see, I had rejected God. Now I wanted to call on His Name—how was I to do it? how was I to come? what was I to say to this God? I almost gave up, but I felt prompted to open the book of testimonies, and it fell open at the testimony of a drunkard; and at the end of his testimony, was his prayer. I believe it was the only prayer that was recorded in that book. 'Jesus, be merciful to me a sinner, and come into my heart, and be my Saviour.'

Friends, I want to tell you, with my whole heart I prayed that prayer. I cried out to God for mercy. I cried out to God for salvation. And I don't know what time I got up from my knees. But I do know this: when I got off my knees, I was a child of God. My sins which were many were all forgiven. I felt so clean. I felt so good. Never did I believe that such peace and joy could be mine as it was in that moment. Never did I think that Jesus could be so real and so near to me. I felt He was so near that if I had put my hand out I could have touched Him.

What a transformation! I knew I was a child of God. I knew that I would never, ever be the same again from that moment. Isn't that wonderful? I knew the old life was over; a new life had begun. I didn't understand it, but I enjoyed the experience of it. I knew that I'd entered into a new dimension of life that I'd never touched before. And it was wonderful. Jesus became a living, bright reality to me. I wanted the world to hear: He lives! I wanted the world to know: He saves! He heals! Folks, listen to me: in that moment not only was I saved, I was healed of many hurts, many wounds, many scars. I was totally set free from all my drink problem, from all the depression. It was a full redemption. From the crown of my head to the soles of my feet, Jesus made me whole. Do I look depressed? I tell you, it was the most wonderful moment of my life, as I stepped out of bondage—oh, if you've been there you'll know what I mean—into liberty. Out of darkness into the glorious light of the gospel. I almost felt the chains fall off my arms. I almost felt the hand of God on my head. It was tremendous.[1]

And I ran down those stairs at nine o'clock that morning, and I said to the manager, 'I'm leaving this place.' 'Why?' 'I'm a Christian now.'

And he laughed. He said, 'Come on, sober up.' I said, 'I was never more sober in all my life. I'm telling you, I'm a

Christian now.'

He said, 'I don't believe you. You're the biggest rogue that ever worked in this bar. You steal and you lie'—and it's true, I did. I said, 'But that's all changed.' 'When did you become a Christian?' he asked. 'At two o'clock this morning,' I replied.

'Now I know you're a liar,' he said. 'There's not a church open at two o'clock in the morning.' I said, 'I wasn't at church.' 'Then,' he said, 'if you weren't at church, how could you become a Christian?'

'I prayed this prayer,' and I repeated the prayer to him. And he started to cry.

'Hey,' I said, 'do you want to be a Christian?' He said, 'I am a Christian—I go to church every Sunday.' I thought, 'Boy, if I'm a rogue you're a bigger rogue!' I said, 'Well, I don't know about that, but I know I'm a Christian.'

He said, 'Look, we'll put you to the test.' 'What do you mean by "test"?' He said, 'You work here one more week, and we'll find out if you're true or false. Okay?'

I was going to say, 'No, no way will I work here one more week,' when I remembered the word of the young evangelist. He had said, 'John, Jesus not only saves, but He keeps. You will be kept by the power of God.' And folks, let me tell you something now. This is my testimony. In those few hours of my new-found faith, I planted my feet on the word of God. Amen? Amen? Not my feelings, not my intellect, thank God, but the word of God. I believed the word of God, that I'd be kept by the power of God. I said, 'Yes, I'll work that week.'

What a week that was! I would not like to go through it again. But I've got news for you: I did go through it. You know why? Because God's word can not be broken. Isn't that wonderful? What God says He does. What God promises He gives. And 'He is not a man that He should lie.' And I was kept, and I am still being kept thirty-five years later; I am still being kept by the power of God.

Folks would come and say, 'Hey, is it true what they're saying about you?' Oh, the manager had got to them, 'He's away, he's gone hallelujah!' So they would come in and say, 'Hey! is it true what they're saying about you?'

'Why, what are they saying?'

'You know, you've joined the Salvation Army—is that right? You're a Christian.'

I said, 'That's right, I am a Christian.'

'And you believe this?' (and they brought a great big Bible into the pub this night) 'You believe this?'

I said, 'Of course I do' (I hadn't even read it yet!)—'of course I believe it.'

Let me tell you, this was a sore point. Do you know that the first morning after I got converted I had to go and buy a Bible? I had all those Bibles in my mother's cupboard and I had to go and buy one! I'm telling you, for a Scotsman that was a hard thing.

Anyway, I said, 'Of course I believe it.' 'You believe this?' and they were getting the Bible open. 'It's full of prostitutes and homosexuals—it's pornography!' They were tearing the pages out of it. And I thought, 'This is too much.' They said, 'You really believe it?' I said, 'Of course I believe it.' 'Okay then, you believe the word of God?' 'I believe the word of God.' 'Right, turn that water into wine.' Oh, I tell you! 'Hey, John the Baptist, come 'ere!' I think that was prophetic!

I went upstairs that night and said, 'O God, I'll never make it. I'll never make it. They're too much for me—I don't have the answers—too much for me, Lord.'

Right there in that room, God spoke. God spoke these words.

'Son, I'll never leave you, and I'll never forsake you. I'll never, never let go your hand.'

Had it been audible, it could not have been stronger. As a

matter of fact, I thought it was an audible voice. I looked round—and there was no-one in that room. And when I discovered that's what God spoke—I didn't even know it was in the Bible—when I realised God had spoken these words into my spirit, I fell on my knees in that little room thirty-five years ago, and I said, 'O God, if You will never leave me, I will never leave You. I need You more than You need me.'

Folks, I want to tell you something. He has never broken that promise, through thick and thin, through many deep waters, through many sorrows, through many trials and many tribulations, my God has proved true to His word. 'When you pass through the waters, the rivers shall not overflow you. Though you go through the fire, the flames shall not kindle upon you, for you are precious in My sight.' What a God we have! What a relationship is ours, that we are one with God the Father, and God the Son, and God the Holy Spirit! O that the world would know that Jesus lives, that Jesus saves, that Jesus heals, that Jesus delivers. Out there they need to know it, and you need to know it too. He's here, He's here. And He is the same yesterday, today, and forever, unchanging. I went through that week, not just somehow, but triumphantly. And God brought me through.

And all throughout Edinburgh it spread like wildfire: 'Half-Pint has gone hallelujah!' And the pub crowd all came to see the great sight—what a sight it was. A great big Thompson Chain Reference, and I didn't even know where Genesis was. And they said, '*You?* the *Bible?* Aw, come on, we'll give you a week' (wasn't that generous?)—'We'll give you a week and you'll be back with the old crowd again.'

It's been a long week; it's been thirty-five years. I hope they're not holding their breath.

They said, 'You must be off your head.' And I said, 'Well, if I'm off my head I must be on my feet, and that's where I'm meaning to stay.' And they came back the next week, and the next, and the next, and I can't remember how many more they came back. But they finally said (not me), 'You're a real hallelujah!' Wasn't that a good testimony? 'You're a real hallelujah!' And that was it; they had gone.

Note

[1] Mr. Hamilton had suffered fearfully in his early days in ways to which he seldom refers. The healing of the wounds was nothing short of a miracle. — H.B.B.

13

The First Convert

But my best friend Stewart was in hospital, and I went to see him in the Royal Infirmary in Edinburgh. I wanted to tell him what Jesus had done in my life. And I told him what I've told you, maybe not in the same detail, but I told him. And his wife was sitting, and as I went on telling him, she was getting angrier and angrier, and finally she couldn't contain herself.

'You! you're no good. You're just no good, and you'll never change. A leopard will never change its spots, and that's what you are. You've just been no good for my husband. You're just no good.'

'Agnes, that is all changed.' But I could not convince her. You see, there are some people you'll never convince.

But my friend lying in that bed, who had never been in a church in his life, said: 'John, don't laugh when I tell you this.' 'What is it, Stewart?' He said, 'All my life—*all my life*—I've wanted to be a Christian.' I wonder where the Christians were who could have told him. I said, 'Stewart, you can be a Christian now.'

His wife said, 'Don't be so silly! how can my husband get out of bed and go to church!' I said, 'He doesn't have to get out of bed and go to church.'

He asked, 'What do you have to do?' I said, 'All you have to do is pray, Stewart.'

She said, 'You're not going to pray here, are you?'

I said, 'Look, you've just said he can't get out of his bed—where else can we pray?'

She said, 'If you're going to pray here, I'm going out.' Isn't that sad? You think of that. She was angry because her husband, who was in hospital (although only for a minor operation), wanted to pray. And they call this a Christian country! She said, 'If you pray, I'm going out.'

He said, 'I want to pray.'

She said, 'I'm going.'

I said, 'Praise the Lord!' And I was so glad—oh, she marched out that ward so angry—but I was so happy: my best pal was going to pray that prayer! I got on my knees at his bedside and I said, 'Stewart, pray this prayer.'

And you know, it was a very busy and a very noisy ward. But when the nurses saw that I was on my knees with this young man, they just stood still for a moment. And the patients were just quiet. And all you heard were two men praying. 'Lord Jesus, be merciful to me a sinner, and come into my heart and be my Saviour.' And I felt Stewart's tears on the back of my hand. I said, 'Stewart, how do you feel?'

He said, 'Hey, I feel as though I've been in a washing machine, I feel so clean! I feel so good!'

I said, 'You're a Christian now!' He said, 'Yes!' I said, 'Yeah! join the club, you're in! You get out of that bed, and you and I will evangelise Edinburgh!' Small ambitions! 'We'll get out there and we'll tell them all about Jesus.' I said, 'See you next week.' I was so happy. My best pal was my first convert. My feet hardly touched the ground; I walked out there on air.

I soon came down to earth, for there she was standing at the door.

'Agnes, you'll never guess.'

'What is it?' 'Stewart's a Christian now.' 'Oh,' she said, 'you make me sick.' And looking at her I could have been sick! She said, 'Who do you think you are—Billy Graham?' I said, 'I'm not Billy Graham, but I'm telling you—look, don't take my word for it. You go and ask him, he'll tell you.' 'We'll see,' she said. Oh, and I stood there and I thought, 'Oh, what a shock she's going to get. What a real shock when he tells her.' And I stood and I watched her go right down to where his bed was.

* * * * *

He never told her. He never spoke a word to her. He never said he prayed, he never said he asked Jesus into his life, not a word did he speak. Do you know why? do you know why? He was dead.

She called out, 'Oh, Stewart, you've gone!'

'Yes, Agnes, Stewart's gone, to be with Jesus.'

Isn't that wonderful? Had he waited one more moment, or till the next day, he'd be in hell. Let me just remind you: he had never, never been in church in his life; never heard a sermon; never heard a prayer...until that day. And that day he said, 'I'm coming. I'm coming.'

How many of you have heard the gospel many times? how many services have you attended? how many people have prayed for you? I want to ask you, are you saved? are you born again? As I looked at that young man who just a few minutes earlier had prayed that prayer, before the doctors and nurses came and put the screens round him, God planted a truth into my heart that day, and it's this: a simple truth, but I want you to hear it. *Tomorrow does not belong to man: only today.* Do you hear that? *Tomorrow does not belong to us, only today.* And today if you will hear His voice, harden not your heart. For behold, *now* is the accepted time. Behold, *now* is the day of salvation.

And I walked away from that ward with a prayer in my heart: 'O God, wherever I am and wherever I go, let this be my testimony, that today is the accepted time for all men. And let me not be ashamed to tell it, because for some tomorrow could be too late.'

Today He can be your Saviour. Tomorrow he might be your Judge. 'Choose you this day whom you will serve: but as for me and my house, we will serve the Lord.'

14

Finding Fellowship

In those very early days of my new-found faith, it seemed there was born in me a tremendous hunger for the Word of God. I just loved the Bible, the book that I detested as a wee boy in Sunday School, this book that was given to me every year for perfect attendance at Sunday School, when I wanted not a Bible but a story book. I don't know that it was wise to start at Genesis, but that's where I started. I didn't know any better. I thought, well, to read, you've got to start at the beginning. And I ploughed my way through, because I loved the Author of the book. I loved Jesus with a passion that was almost an agony. And it seemed that hymn was in reality my life:

> Heaven above is softer blue,
> Earth around is sweeter green;
> Something lives in every hue
> Christless eyes have never seen.
> Birds with gladder songs o'erflow,
> Flowers with deeper beauties shine,
> Since I know, as now I know
> I am His and He is mine.

And oh, what a tremendous relationship it was. What a tremendous walk with Jesus I had. I don't think my feet touched the ground. Every day brought new revelations of His love, and new manifestations of His power. His presence was rich. And everywhere I went I told people about Jesus.

And you know, I wanted to find a spiritual home—because I don't believe God wants us to be spiritual tramps. I lived in Edinburgh at that time, and Edinburgh, as you'll know, has a church at nearly every street corner. I went to the nearest one and then worked my way right round. Some scared me, some left me cold, and of some I thought, 'I'll never go back there again.' But you know, there came a desire to belong. I wanted to belong to a family of God. I wanted to belong to a place where I could not only receive, but give, and support.

I remember one morning praying (I didn't go out to church that morning; I just had a time on my own, and I prayed)—I said, 'Father, please show me, please show me where You would have me worship and serve You.'

And I'll never forgot it. I went out in the evening at six o'clock, really believing that God would show me in that hour the very place where I should be. And I'll never forget: walking up that street, I had just gone a couple of hundred yards from where I lived, and there was old Anne.

She was seventy, just saved three or four years earlier. I tell you, that woman was on fire. You touched it and you got singed. There she was standing with a great handful of gospel tracts. I was walking up the road and she was standing just outside the church.

And she said, 'Excuse me, sir, would you like a gospel tract?'

'I'd love one.'

She nearly fell off the pavement. And then, I think because I said that, she got a wee bit more bold and went on.

'We're having a service tonight. Would you like to come

into the service?'

'I would be delighted.' By this time I almost had to get the smelling salts out!

And do you know, when I walked through that door, I knew that this was my home. Isn't that a marvellous thing? Isn't it a marvellous knowledge to have, that you know where you ought to be? And I tell you, they were a motley crew; there were all kinds there. But I'll never forget the singing, and I'll never forget the fellowship; I'll never forget the warmth I felt as I sat there that night. I listened to the minister: he was a Mr Robertson from the Congregational Church; he was a blind man. But oh, he knew the Word of God. He had a great big shock of white hair, and he stood about ten feet tall, and he thundered the gospel. And of course anyone behind me got nothing, because I drank it all in. I was just so hungry for the Word of God.

And you know, as it often happens, soon you come alongside someone of like mind; and there was a young man called Gordon—he just seemed to be the right kind for me. He was just so on fire for God.

It was a common thing to have all-night prayer meetings, fasting, street evangelism, door-to-door visitation. I've never been in a church like it, so active for the things of God. And I'm so glad that was the church God allowed me to move into, because I could never have lived in a church that was half-hearted, or cold, or lukewarm. It was just the very church that I needed, the very people that I needed. And you know, as I read the Word, and the hunger grew for God, and the desire to serve Him became again like an agony, young Gordon and I went out to the little country villages, and we preached the gospel, just the two of us—we went round the doors telling people about Jesus.

It was a wonderful time. And I was in no way looking for anything more than I had. I thought I had received everything in salvation. My feet hadn't touched the ground.

15

There Comes the Baptism

One day, as I met Gordon, I knew something different had happened to him.

I said, 'Gordon, what's happened to you?'

He said, 'It's the Baptism.'

I said, 'What? It's done that for you, the Baptism? I'll see the minister next Sunday, and I'll get baptised.'

I thought he was speaking about water baptism; I thought, 'My goodness, if water baptism has done that for you, it's time I got baptised in water.'

'John, it's not that kind of baptism.' You see, I was so ignorant. I said, 'What kind is it?' He said, 'It's the Baptism in the Holy Ghost.'

And I said, 'Can I have it?' 'Of course you can.'

'Well, tell me, what do I do?' I thought maybe I had to go to a Bible School or something—I don't know. I said, 'What do I do to get this Baptism in the Holy Spirit?'

'All you have to do is pray,' he said.

'Come on, then, let's pray!' Oh, I tell you! He said, 'We can't pray in Princes Street; we'll need to go to the church.' I said, 'Well, let's go to the church then.'

It was about half-past eleven at night, I remember it well.

And we got down on our knees and started to pray. And you know, he always prayed loud, and I prayed loud. And many people complained; they said, 'What are you shouting for? God's not deaf.' And we always used to say, 'But he's not nervous either.' And so we shouted and we prayed, 'O God!' And then, just as he was praying in this little old vestry in the church, suddenly he came out with this beautiful tongue.

Well, I shouldn't say it was beautiful—I was petrified. I thought, 'This guy's gone bananas—what's happened to him?' And I went over to him and I shook him.

'Gordon, what's wrong with you?' I didn't say, 'What's right with you?' I said, 'What's wrong with you?'

And as I'm shaking him...I looked at his face. And believe me, his face was shining. And I remember saying to God, 'I want that...but I don't want this.' I didn't understand it. And as I shook him, he said, 'What's wrong?' I said, 'You tell me: what's all this gibberish?'

He didn't say, 'That's tongues,' or 'It's in the Bible,' He just said, 'That's the Baptism.' I said, 'That's the Baptism? No, thank you. I don't want that Baptism.' And all he said in response to that was, 'John, don't let the devil get in.' I said, 'You're too late. He's in with both feet.'

And for the first time, folks (that was the one-year stage), for the first time I experienced warfare, battle, whatever you like to call it. Suddenly it seemed that there were two powers at work in my life now. And when that young man said, 'Don't let the devil get in'—I tell you, right from that moment I turned to Jesus, I wanted to be a fighter for God. I didn't want to be mealy-mouthed and weak-kneed and spineless. I wanted Him to get the best of my life, for He'd given the best for me. When my friend said, 'Don't let the devil get in,' I said, 'Well, what do I do?' He said, 'Just get back down on your knees and start praying again.'

And of course I got back down. I don't know whether he

prayed for me, I don't know if he laid hands on me. All I know is that my hands shot up. And I cried out to God: 'O God! baptise me in the Holy Ghost.'

Suddenly the heavens were opened. And I want to describe the experience as it happened. Suddenly there came the mighty power of the Holy Ghost into that room, so mighty and so powerful that I was thrown bodily right across that room, not once but many times. And I tell you, friends, that little room was like a battle-field. And not one part of my body was hurt or in any way damaged, and yet I was thrown right across that room, as I have said, not once, but many times. And I was in a very unusual state; I was laughing and crying at the same time. My face was just soaked with tears. And all I wanted to say was, 'Jesus, I love You!' And out poured this beautiful language in tongues. Oh, I tell you, I loved Jesus in that moment...words could not describe the love that was poured in at that moment. Words could never describe the power. It was like electricity going right through my body. And that was at twelve o'clock.

Do you know when we left that little vestry? Eight o'clock in the morning. I still couldn't speak English...I maybe still can't speak it very well, but you know what I mean? I still couldn't speak English! And I was going to this job, this shop where I worked. I thought, 'Lord, you'll have to help me.'

And boy, I tell you, it was difficult—a lady asked me something and I just turned round to speak and it was tongues that came out. She jumped about six feet in the air. And she screamed, and the manager came round and said, 'What's the matter, madam?' 'Oh, it's not me,' she said. 'It's this young man.'

He said, 'John, what's wrong with you?' And I tried to speak again and it was tongues that came out and he said, 'Don't come near me! You go home; you're sick.' I had my

157

own feelings but I couldn't even say what I felt. He said, 'Excuse me, madam, he's just got a little bit religion, but he'll be all right.' And he sent me home for the whole day. And I spent that day praising God, at his expense! It made it doubly worthwhile.

But that night was the prayer meeting—the church prayer meeting. I couldn't wait to get to this prayer meeting. I thought, 'Won't the minister be glad when he hears what happened to me?' H'm! We got into that little prayer meeting. And I don't know what you do here, but let me just encourage you to get back to your knees again when you pray. That's how I was brought in, on my knees. And there they were on their knees. And the minister was on his knees, at his usual place; and I pushed a man away to get next to the minister—I wanted him to be the first to hear what God had done for me. And my knees had hardly touched the floor before I was speaking in tongues. He put his hand on my shoulder and almost dislocated it.

He said, 'You're not bringing that in here. That is of the devil.' I said, 'What? of the *devil*? then I don't want it.' He said, 'You're not splitting my church up'—I hadn't even thought about splitting his church. And I thought, 'What is happening? what—?'

I couldn't understand it: now there was a division, and I could feel it. And it hurt me, because I loved these people, I loved them: they were my brothers and sisters in Christ. And I could not get through to them that this was what God had given me. I didn't have the language to explain it to them. I didn't have the knowledge of the Bible to tell them. I didn't even know it was *in* the Bible. I just knew that God had met with me in a dynamic way, and my friend Gordon said it was the Baptism in the Spirit. That's all I knew.

And as the minister was pouring his wrath on me, about splitting his church—and it was of the devil—and I wouldn't bring it in here, and so on, one of the deacons stood up and said, 'Just a minute, Mr. Robertson. What does the Bible say?' (I didn't even know the Bible said anything.)

The minister said, 'The Bible says, "Try the spirits, and see if they be of God."'

He said, 'Why don't you do that, then? You can't say that's of the devil if you don't know. *Try* the spirits.' And the minister said to me, 'John, are you prepared for this?'

'Well,' I said, 'truthfully I don't understand it, but I'm prepared for anything that will prove not to you only but to me that what I have is from God. And believe me, if it's not from God, then I don't want it either.' And so we got down on our knees again.

But do you know something that they didn't know? When they said, 'Try the spirits and see if they be of God,' they didn't know that before I gave my life to Jesus, I sat under one of the finest clairvoyants in Edinburgh, and she wanted to train me to be a clairvoyant. I was deep in spiritism before I gave my life to Jesus. And when they said, 'Try the spirits and see if they be of God,' in my ignorance and foolishness I thought they were really saying, 'Get back into spiritism, and we'll soon see if God will bring you out of that.' Now you may think that's strange, but that was exactly what I felt and how I understood it.

So we got down on our knees. And God did a wonderful thing, friends. I got on my knees before Him, and I forgot all the people round about. I was once again in pure praise and worship before my God. A new dimension of praise and worship had opened up to me. A new dimension of worship had broken upon my spirit. And I tell you, it was glorious. But then, the time came when they put their hands on my shoulder (this time it was a bit more gentle) and Mr. Robertson said, 'Tell me, brother, is Jesus Christ coming back in the flesh, or is He coming back in the spirit?'

And without a moment's hesitation I said, 'Oh, praise

God, He's coming back in the flesh.'

And that deacon who had stood by me, right there and then was baptised in the Holy Ghost, singing in tongues—not a hand laid on him, not a prayer offered.

And the minister said, 'Pray for me that I might receive.' I said, 'I can't pray for you—you're my minister!' He said, 'I command you to pray for me,' and I said 'Oh-h-h....'

And nothing happened. Nothing happened.

No, something did happen. He said this, and I want you to hear it tonight; there are some in this gathering, you need to hear this. Don't stop your ears now, have them open to this. He said, 'I can't deny that what you have is from God. I can't deny it. God has baptised you in the Holy Ghost. But,' he said, 'you'll not bring it into this church.' Did you hear that? 'You will not bring it in here.'

Now rightly or wrongly I submitted to that. He was my minister, I was only a new Christian, and the three of us, Gordon, this young deacon and myself, gathered together outwith the church because we were not allowed to express the gift of God.

And so we gathered and prayed together, we worshipped together as the Spirit allowed us to worship; we lifted up our voice in new tongues as we met. It was glorious. But it wasn't balanced. You see, the Spirit is given not to divide, but to unite. And somewhere along the way our fellowship got too close: it got too close. I'm finding it very difficult just to know how much to say. I look to God to give me the right things to share tonight, and I feel led to go a little further into this.

We were a little threesome—and we didn't cut ourselves off from the church: we went to all the activities that the church had; we still poured our lives into the church—but over and above that we met separately, because we were the only people who were baptised in the Spirit. And please remember, young people, this was over thirty years ago.

There were no Charismatic meetings around then. The Pentecostals were on one side, and the others were on the other, and never the twain did meet. Now I never felt led to go anywhere else but this church. God had me there for a purpose, all right. And so we poured our lives into that church, and over and above we met for praise and worship and to help one another in our new-found Baptism in the Holy Spirit.

16

Down to the Pit

And Gordon prayed over me one night; he called it prophecy, but I didn't know what it was. He said it was prophecy, and I believed him. And the prophecy was—and tonight I can feel it as it happened that night—he said, 'You'll go to England. And doors will open up for you, and a work will open up for you. And God will take you into new places there, and you will bring Pentecost to that people.' Are you listening to that tonight? (It just suddenly dawned on me now, that could have been a real prophecy; but the timing was wrong.) And he said, 'You'll go now, and you'll go to that place, for God will open up these doors for you.'

And that's what I did. I left my job, I left my home, and I went down to England. When I got there, of course, not one door opened. Not one. And I was there for about three to four months. Nothing happened. I couldn't even get work; I got nothing. And I was getting to a place of desperation. And somehow, for the first time I just knew, although I didn't understand it, that the presence of God and the Word of God and the place of prayer were not as meaningful to me now as they had been in the beginning before I left Edinburgh. Something had happened. And God was trying to say to me, 'You're in the wrong place. Get back home.' But the little band of Christians kept encouraging me to stay there. And I listened to them, not to God, and I stayed.

And one morning before I came down for my breakfast, God spoke. I'll never forget it. Two words: '*Go home*. Go home.' Now it didn't matter what He said—the thing that thrilled me was, I heard God speak again. And that meant everything to my heart. God had spoken; I was back into right relationship with Him; I heard His voice.

And I ran down the stairs and I said, 'I've just had a word from God.' They said, 'Oh, good, brother, what did He say to you?' I said, 'He's just told me to go home.'

'That's not from God. That's not from God!' I said, 'What do you mean, it's not from God?'

'You know what's wrong with you?' I said, 'No, tell me.'

'Just because the way is tough and the doors are not opening as you want them to open, you're going to give in and go back home. You're not made of the real stuff. There must be an area of pride there.'

I said, 'All right, I'll stay.'

Folks, I knew, I knew the moment I said, 'I'll stay,' that I'd stepped out of the will of God; I knew it.

And just at that very same moment the telephone rang. It was the manager from a shop who had asked for me. And when I came on to the phone I said, 'Yes, what is it?' He said, 'I've changed my mind. You can start tomorrow.'

'Oh,' I said, 'I haven't changed my mind.' He said, 'What do you mean?' I said, 'I told you, I didn't realise when I applied for the job that it was a licensed grocer's, and I told you I wouldn't serve drink—I told you that.'

He said, 'You don't have to serve it.' Isn't Satan subtle? 'You don't have to serve it. I'll put you on to the bacon and the cold meat counter. You just say you'll be there.'

I said, 'Right, I'll take the job.' And I got that job, and I got the applause of the Christians. I got their smile of approval.

But God's face.... God hid His face.

And within six months I was back behind the bar again. I was pulling pints again. I was in the gutter again. God, and the things of God, and the people of God—no longer. And I would never dare try to tell people what those two years were like. But I know, I know that in those two years there came a point in my life (listen, Christian, tonight), there came a point in my life when I sold myself to Satan deliberately, purposefully: I gave myself over to Satan. And I was full of hate, full of bitterness. I was ugly; even the barmen said, 'Jock, go and wash your mouth out.'

Can you understand this tonight? Can you understand how it could be that a man could earlier cry out, 'O God, forgive me,' and in that moment in that little room he was forgiven, he was cleansed, every sin was blotted out, every fetter was broken, every bondage was snapped; he was free as he had never been free before—can you understand it?—and then, in that little vestry, the Holy Ghost had come and the power of the Holy Ghost had been so great his body could not contain it, and through his lips poured forth the new tongue, as the Spirit gave utterance...I had known what it was in those early days to walk with God; I had known what it was to get into that place alone with Him, where He would speak with me face to face, and reveal Himself to me in a way I never thought possible on this side of eternity...and yet, here I was, behind this bar! Oh, that I could tell it! But let it be a warning tonight. Let it be a caution in your life. Let it be a warning, young Christian, tonight! God requires of us obedience, whatever the cost, and whatever the smile or the disapproval of men; He expects and demands and deserves our obedience. And outside of that obedience, there is no place of safety for you: none.

And that's where I was: standing behind a bar again. And

for two years, it was a place of utter darkness. I'm not going to weary you with it. But when it was night, I wished it was morning. And time and time again I tried suicide, to get out of the hell that I was in.

But remember this: God is faithful. Isn't that a beautiful thing? 'As far as the east is from the west, so far has He removed our sins from us. As a Father pitieth His children, so the Lord pities them that fear Him. Cry unto me, Zion, and I will answer thee.'

And back home in that little Congregational church was a people praying for John Hamilton the backslider, fasting and praying. I'm going to tell you something tonight. Even in my backslidden state, even in my darkness, I sensed it. I sensed it. There was never a conversation, ugly as that conversation would be, filthy and unclean as that conversation might be, but someone in that company would mention 'Jesus.' It was like an arrow, a sword, wounding me every time. I had denied Him. I had blasphemed His Name again. And I said, 'I don't know Him.'

But oh, the mercy of God. One day, there came into that bar in England my minister, my blind minister. It was a great big, long bar, and he sat there at the door, and one of the barmen came and said, 'Jock, there's a vicar here wants to see you.' And I looked over and I saw my minister sitting there, and I said, 'I don't know him.' He said, 'Well, he knows you and he's asking for you—you better go and see what he wants.'

I went round the counter over to the door where Mr Robertson was sitting and I said, 'Yes, what can I give you?'

And he was fearless! He grabbed me. He said, 'WHAT IS A CHILD OF GOD DOING IN THIS DEN OF INIQUITY?' And that's how he said it: he didn't whisper, 'What's a child of God doing in a den of iniquity?'

My face was in technicolour. I just pushed his hand away and said, 'Who said I was a child of God? Do you want a

drink or do you not?' I was so *hard*...I wasn't *playing* at
being hard: I *was* hard. Take care, Christian. Be not
deceived: God is not mocked. For what a man sows, he will
reap. And that hardness was there.

He said, 'I'm not leaving this place without you.' I love
this man (not then, I didn't). I said, 'Well, I'm—'...no, I'll
not say what I said. I just left him.

I was serving customers. Then came the owner, not the
manager, but the owner, who owned a string of pubs and
came every month to see how the trade was doing (Don't
you tell me God doesn't hear and God doesn't answer
prayer—I'll not listen to you. God does hear, and God does
answer. But it's not by might, and it's not by power, it's by
His Spirit.)—that ungodly man drew near to me and he
said, 'John, I don't know anything about you, but if I were
you I would go with that man.' (Does that not move you?
You're listening to an act of God in mercy and love and
forgiveness.) 'If I were you, I would go with that man.' I
said, 'You're not me, and I've no intention of going with
him.'

He said, 'You're fired.' I said, 'I'm *what*?' He said 'You're
fired.' I said, 'You're one mug. You'll give me a month's
money now, and I'll walk out of here, and I'll take my trade
right along to the next bar.' He said, 'Just you do that, and
God bless you!' I said, 'That'll be right.'

I went upstairs and I packed my things and a few of his
just for good measure, and I came down—I tell you, I was
angry! There's no man can fight love, isn't that right? and
God is love. And I knew I was losing ground; but I put up a
good fight. Isn't it sad? Fighting against God now: not
fighting for Him, fighting against Him. And I had my bag
and my month's money; I walked round the bar and there
was the minister. 'Praise the Lord!' he said.

I said, 'Look, Mr Robertson, when we leave this pub,
when we get oustide, you'll go your way and I'll go mine,

okay?' He said, 'We'll see.'

I had to take him out, because he was a blind man, and he turned his sightless eyes to me as if he could see. He said, 'John, listen. I want to hear no more of it. You're coming home with me, you're coming back to Scotland.'

And I heard myself saying, 'All right, I'll come; I'll come.' Oh, I wasn't there yet, though. No, no—that was only lip service: 'I'll come.'

'But,' he said, 'we can't go home now. There's a Christian family who have given us hospitality for tonight.' And he said, 'They've gathered a few Christians there already; we better go and see them.'

I walked into that home. And I'll never forget it. They were on their knees: they were praying for *me*, John Hamilton the backslider. They had never met me, they never knew me, but there they were crying to God. And I was as *hard!* I sat there and smoked cigarette after cigarette, as they were crying to God that I might get back to Him again.

The minister just came over and he said, 'John, why don't you stop fighting? Why don't you just lay down your arms? Why don't you just surrender your life to Jesus again?'

And I meant it when I said, 'Mr. Robertson, I want to come back. I want to come back. God knows I want to come back...but I feel *nothing! nothing!* I don't feel anything but guilt.' He said, 'John, take God at His word. If we confess our sin, He is faithful and just to forgive us and to cleanse us.' Friend, I knew it, I knew it. But there was such a battle within; there was such a struggle. I remember just kneeling beside the minister saying, 'All right, I'll come.' And he prayed for me, and I prayed, and they were in ecstasy...I felt nothing. But I just knew, 'If I don't come now, I will *never* come back again. I'll never come again in all my life.'

17

The Long Road Back

And I went home the next morning with my minister, back
into that church again—all night prayer meetings, street
evangelism, door-to-door visitation, days of fasting and
praying. And I went through it all: for six months I did it;
and I never once felt the presence of God. Never once. I
witnessed, I prayed, I read my Bible, I fasted, I did all the
things that I did before. But, friends, listen to me tonight:
God in that time never allowed one part of feeling—His
Word only. And His Word never failed. I hope you're
listening tonight. *God wants to wean His Church back to the
Word*—away from the gimmicks of men, away from the
trivialities of the Church, back to the unadulterated, pure
Word of God. Are you listening to me? We have got hooked
on so many things today, and the Word is neglected; and it's
the Word that gives life, it's the Word that gives power, it's
the Word that causes us to stand and not fall. Say Amen to
that. It's His Word. But oh, God didn't leave me there, and
He won't leave you there either. He will do mighty works
within His people. And tonight He's going to do mighty
works in this hall. I know it, I know it.

And I went up the road to the prayer meeting one night—

still with no felt sense of His presence, but I never missed a prayer meeting; I went to every prayer meeting, all night prayer meetings as well. And I'll never forget that night, friends. I walked up that street that night to go to the prayer meeting, and had I not got into the hall when I did, I would have been prostrate on the street. The power of God fell again!

The power of God fell again—are you listening to me? An open Heaven! And God by His love and mercy poured out upon this life again the floods of His Spirit. And I can remember the minister saying (because I was prostrate on the floor, and the people had gathered for prayer), 'We better leave John, we better leave John alone.' And they all moved out of that hall. I don't know where they went to. All I know is, I was before God...before the Throne of God. And friends, it was there revelation after revelation poured out from the Throne. And I tell you, it was real. And strange as it might seem to you tonight, with such an encounter with God, and brought into almost the Holy of Holies as I remember it, the new tongue that God gave me on that morning in the church was not there. It was not there. But I got up out of that hall, and I knew the call of God was on my life: clear, clear call of God to rise up and follow Him.

And I went home in the early hours of that morning. By this time my parents were divorced. Now the first thing I had done when I got saved was to go back and find my mother and my family. I found them, and I said, 'I'm the breadwinner from now on; I'll look after you,' and I did. And now I went back into that same home and I said, 'Mother, God has called me.' She said, 'What do you mean, He's called you?' She was not a Christian, just a lovely old mother. 'What do you mean, He's called you?' I said, 'He wants me to go into Bible College. He wants me to be a missionary, evangelist.' 'How much is He going to pay you?' I said, 'Funny! you've got it wrong! they're not going to pay me, I've got to pay them.' 'And where are you going to get the money from?' And I said, 'God will provide.'

And listen to what she said (remember, there were four of us at that time). She said, 'Listen'—I said, 'Listen, mother, I'm telling you I'm going to Bible College. God has called me; I'm going. And as He provides my needs, I know He'll provide yours.' Now don't be angry with her. She was out scrubbing floors (do you hear me?)—she was out scrubbing floors to keep the family together, and I had been working to make sure we would be kept together. And she said, 'Do you mean to say that you're going to walk out and leave me? Do you know what this means to me?—that I've got to go out and do more work, more scrubbing?' Oh, young people, there's no easy way to follow Jesus. I haven't found it—I haven't found it.

And I went back into my room and I said, 'O God, You've heard my mother's cry. Is this really Your call on my life?'

And God in His graciousness spoke again the very word He had given me in that hall that morning. I said, 'Thank you, Father. And whatever it costs, whatever it takes, I'll follow You.' They were no glib words: I meant every word.

And my mother said to me, 'Have you changed your mind?' I said, 'No, mother, I haven't. I'm going.' 'Well,' she said, 'When you go out that door, don't you ever come back. You're no son of mine. Do you know what the Bible says?' I said, 'No, what does the Bible say?' (I haven't found it; I've been thirty years looking for it and I haven't found it.) She said, 'Charity begins at home.' And I told her: 'Mother, look, please believe me.' She said, 'I don't believe you. All I know is that I've got to work harder, and you're walking out on me. May God forgive you,' she said. Was that easy—to walk out?'

But what made it harder: the church didn't believe me

either, that God had called me. 'Your place is at home! You're going to spoil your testimony. You can't walk out and leave your mother to feed these children, to work harder. Who do you think you are?' I said, 'Please—look, stop! I've told you, God has called me.' Do you know what they did? Do you know what they did? They had a special prayer meeting against the will of God for my life. I know where I'm at tonight, for I know who's kept me there! Every week they prayed, 'O God, open John's eyes. Open his ears. Bring him back into Your will again.' I stopped going to the prayer meeting. How would you like to be going to a prayer meeting where they were praying against the will of God for your life?

I went to the Faith Mission College with not a penny in my pocket, knowing that God had called me there. And, friends, I want to tell you: God provided every need. Every need, right to a razor blade. That's my God.

And one day, God just showed me that I should go back home and speak to my mother. 'But,' I said, 'Lord, the door's shut.' God said, 'I'll open it.'

I lived in Edinburgh and the college was in Edinburgh, and so I had to take a bus. And I saw a dear old lady, Mrs. Murray, a real, good, old supporter of the Mission. And she said, 'Hullo, brother, where are you going?' I said, 'I'm going home.' 'How's college doing?' I said, 'Marvellous' (which was a lie), 'marvellous. Oh,' I said, 'Here's my bus, I better get on it.' I'll never forget this woman. She always had bundles of tracts; she was always out witnessing to people. 'God bless you, son,' and I thought she put a bundle of tracts into my hands. And I sat on the bus, and I said, 'O God, give me the grace to give these tracts out'...God's man for God's hour! 'Give me the grace to give these tracts out.'

I opened my eyes, and there was a pile of notes; I think there was £20 or £25—and that was a lot of money then.

And I wept on that bus. I said, 'Lord, she needs it more than I do.' And yet I had peace about it; it was all right.

So I walked up to my home, and I think mother must have seen me through the curtains (you ladies are experts at looking through curtains!). And I knocked on the door and she didn't open it; she said, 'What do you want?' I said, 'I want in.'

'I told you, you don't belong here!'

Oh, doesn't God have a sense of humour! He doesn't need to give you wisdom in such an hour!

I said, 'If you don't want Mrs Quin to hear what I've got to say to you, you better open that door.'

She pulled me in right away! I tell you, He's a very practical God. 'In you come,' she said, and she brought me into the sitting-room. And she always called me Big Boy when she was trying to be sarcastic. She said, 'Well, Big Boy, how are you doing?' I said, 'You see me—overfed and underpaid.'

'Do you remember your words before you left here?' I said, 'What did I say to you?' 'Oh, you've forgotten them already?' I said, 'Tell me—what did I say?'

'Oh, you told me that God would provide your need and God would provide my need, isn't that right?' And I said, 'Yes, mother, that is what I told you.'

She went to the dresser. Now listen to what she said:

'Well, you tell me, or you tell your God, where am I going to get £25 to pay that bill?'

I said, 'There it is.'

She ran through to her bedroom; she didn't know what to do with herself. She'd met with a miracle and she couldn't face up to it. And she called, 'Come in here quick.' And I ran and there she was on her knees at her bedside: 'I want Jesus to come into my life. I want *Jesus* to come into my life.' And I had the joy of pointing my mother to Christ. And she got up off her knees and she boasted to everybody,

'My son's an evangelist! He's just like Billy Graham!' What God can do! and what God has done!

Note

[1] This is peculiarly poignant in view of earlier circumstances to which Mr Hamilton did not refer in detail on the occasion of this sermon. He was born a sickly child and had been expected to die as an infant. The doctor did all he could but felt there was really no hope. He even offered to relieve the mother's problem by adopting the child and taking him abroad and giving him the most suitable foods, etc. Mrs Hamilton would not give up 'her bairn' and the doctor made one further suggestion—that she take the babe out in the early hours of the morning when the air would be at its purest. This she did as she went scrubbing stairs to support her family. Now it must have seemed to her that John had turned his back on her. Her pain must have been great.

18

In Harness at Last

I went out into the work of the Faith Mission. And I've said on many platforms, and I say it again here tonight: I thank God for those years. I thank God for the school that He took me through in those seven years of trusting more fully in Him, not leaning on the energy of the flesh, not depending on men. Oh, I could fill a book with such stories. [You're doing not bad, John, not bad at all!—H.B.B.]

Let me just tell you one very quickly. We were in this little caravan, with nothing in the cupboard. (That wouldn't harm me now, but then it did harm me.) We cried to God—this wee lad Tommy Shaw said, 'Brother, what are we going to do?' I said, 'We're going to pray and ask God to send it.' And we cried aloud. We were crying so loud we never heard the caravan door getting knocked. And after we'd spent ourselves in prayer, I said, 'How about a wee cup of tea?' 'Aye,' he said, 'Why don't you go and fill the kettle then?' And we opened the door. And, believe me, there was a box on the caravan steps, full of good things— full of good things! KitKats, and...oh, boy! Sausages and beans...everything. And, I tell you, we enjoyed every part of it.

But God rebuked me, and God said, 'You would cry as loud for such food because you're hungry. And out there they're dying without the Bread of Life. Have you ever cried as loud for them?' Are you listening, Christian?

Three days later, there came another knock on the caravan door, and this lady was standing there. We invited her in and asked her who she was. And she said, 'I was just passing by and I saw your little banner, 'Faith Mission Campaign.' She told us that her husband was lying seriously ill in hospital and she had been visiting him. And she said, 'I saw your banner and I thought, I must give this Mission something—I'll buy a box of groceries. But,' she said, 'I knocked on your door, and you didn't hear me. But I heard your prayers. And,' she said, 'I just left them.' 'Oh,' we said, 'are you the lady?' And she said, 'Yes, I am.'

I said, 'Well, what made you come to us?' 'As a wee girl, two Pilgrims came to our village, and I heard the gospel for the first time through them, and I gave my life to Jesus.' And she said, 'I would like to tell you that I went on and on with Jesus, but I didn't.' That day she came back. Oh, what joy in bringing men and women to Jesus. Isn't it a wonderful joy? There's no greater joy!

In my first year in the Faith Mission I met my wife Zillah. We first met briefly and just knew that God had brought us together, and that we should marry. And God in His own wonderful way provided and opened a door whereby we could do what He asked.

19

A Church of His Own

After seven years I left the Faith Mission and went into the United Free Church of Scotland as a minister in Gorebridge. And I never, never had such a challenge in all my life as that first church. I couldn't really take time to tell you the whole story tonight. But let me tell you this. God promised me revival for that church. And at the end of my first year, my deacons and the congregational board all came together and said, 'It's no use, Mr. Hamilton. The doors will close. There's no change here.' And one man said, 'You know what's wrong? We're getting too much religion. We're getting too much of the gospel. We need something secular.' O God, I thought, they haven't heard what I've been saying in this last year. 'We need some dances and some concerts —that'll bring the money in—that'll bring the people in.'

It was a long, long hill up to our house from the church. And I walked up that hill, my feet dragging. I walked in and Zillah said, 'What's wrong with you?' I told her. She said, 'What are you going to do?' I said, 'There's only one thing I can do, and that's get before God.'

I called the little group of Christians who were there— just a handful—to prayer. And every night we prayed. But there was one young man, Ronnie Graham, who said, 'Mr. Hamilton, I'll pray with you through the night, if you want.' I said, 'Ronnie, we'll do that.' I want you to listen to me tonight. For six weeks—six weeks unbroken—we called upon the Name of the Lord. We cried to God for that situation. And I'll never forget it. We prayed, we read the Word, had a cup of tea, went back to prayer, back to the Word—and that young man left my house every morning to go to work without having slept. Such was the burden for the church that was in our hearts.

And there came an hour I'll never forget. After we had just had a cup of tea, we got back down to pray again. He knelt beside me. And suddenly, without a hand being laid on him, he poured out in new tongues. And my immediate reaction was to stop him. I put my hand on him to say, 'Ronnie, don't touch it, don't touch that.' But when I put my hand on his shoulder, I heard myself encouraging him: 'Go right in, Ronnie! You're being baptised in the Holy Ghost! Hallelujah! you're being baptised in the Holy Ghost.'

And as I said that, the new tongue for the first time after many years came flooding through my lips again.

Listen, Christian: the heavens were opened! And from that moment I just knew that that church would never be the same again. And instead of having dances and concerts, I went back down to my committee and said, 'We're going to have a Faith Mission Campaign.' It was the only Mission I knew, the Faith Mission. 'We're going to have a Faith Mission Campaign.' And out of that campaign there are people on the mission field today, there are people in the ministry today, out of that one campaign. God began to move, and God began to work. People were baptised in the Holy Ghost.

But let me tell you—because I owe a lot to Mr. Black here and Miss Taylor. At that time, it was quite unique for any minister outside the Pentecostal churches to be baptised in the Holy Ghost. And word got round—I forget the man from Glasgow who sent me a letter inviting me to come to a Pentecostal Leaders' meeting. I went there. And I tell you, I was disgusted: it was as dead and as barren! I said, 'Lord, what am I doing here? I thought I was going to come into a place of life!' They were speaking about this problem and the next problem: 'What are we going to do? what are we not going to do?'

But then in the afternoon they had a speaker called Mr. Black. And I sat there, and I was so fed up with the whole day's proceedings; I thought, 'I wonder what this man's going to say.'

Friend, listen: I sat there and I wept. For this was what my heart hungered for. This was my heart's desire: to hear a man stand up and preach the Word of God under the anointing of the Holy Ghost. And I remember getting my diary out and saying, 'I must get this man for my Saturday night meeting.' And I went to him after the meeting and I said, 'Brother! You fed my soul. Oh, I needed to hear that today. And, as a matter of fact, I'd like you to come to my church in Gorebridge.' 'Well,' he said, 'I don't carry my diary with me. But if you care to get in touch with me, we'll see what we can do. Right?'

And I went home and I said, 'Zillah—oh, Zillah, you want to meet this man. Oh, I've arrived—I know now what God is saying, what God's going to do, in this place. I've got the very man.'

And a week passed. A second week passed. A third week passed, and she said, 'You haven't phoned that man.' I said, 'No, leave me. Leave me.' Something was happening; I didn't understand it, but I didn't want to phone. Little did I realise all that God was going to do through this man. Little did I realise that Satan was putting up a fight again.

But then I went to another Pentecostal Leaders' meeting. This time I took one or two of my elders. And we decided not to go to the business side of it, but just go to the preaching side. And the chairman stood up and said, 'We're sorry, the preacher expected couldn't come this afternoon. But you'll be delighted to hear that Mr. Black has agreed to speak at short notice'—oh, no!

But once he stood up to preach, I forgot all about my negligence, and I was fed again through the anointed word.

But I tried to hide from him. Can you imagine? I tried to hide from him. And we had our tea in this little place. And I said to this young fellow that was with me, 'Let's go out for a walk.' And he said, 'Are you all right?'—because I never go for a walk. I remember Mr. Black was sitting on the other side, and I made for the door. Guess what? he was right in front of me. How he managed it I'll never know. I had looked and thought, 'I'm safe, I'll get out that door.'

'Oh,' he said, 'There you are, young man' (towering over me). 'You know, you never got in touch with me.' And oh, all the lies that poured out—'Oh, yes, I've been busy, and I've—' (you know).

And he said, 'Well, if you've got your diary there, I've got my diary tonight.' I thought, 'My, he's desperate to preach at my church.' And I remember opening my diary, and I was *ashamed:* there wasn't a date on it! 'Oh,' he said, 'I think I can come any Saturday.' And so we arranged when to come.

(Will you forget that day, Mr. Black?) They were baptised in the Holy Ghost, right, left and centre. Never had we a day like it. One man walked through the glass door; he didn't know where he was; we had to redirect him: 'Come on, it's this way, Joe.' God came in, God began to move. And it was from that moment we got acquainted with Struthers, and you dear people here.

And I want to say from my heart, I've thanked the Lord again and again for opening that door to this fellowship. It has meant much to me down through the years, and I truly have valued the ministry of Miss Taylor, her words of wisdom, words of knowledge, over my life, at crisis after crisis. And I thank God for Mr. Black.

But God was moving. And God moved us on and on, and we went from one church to another. And to every church we went, we brought not only the gospel, but the Baptism in the Holy Ghost. Into places that were barren, traditional, God began to move. For God gave me on that morning revelation after revelation of what He would do in my life. And God has kept His word. I was confronted with people with needs. I didn't ask God for gifts. All I asked God was to meet the needs of those who stood before me. And God wonderfully, mightily delivered, healed, baptised, sent people out with the call of God upon their lives. I tell you, this gospel is good news—it's good news. It makes men whole again, and it gives men hope out of despair; and it brings them out of darkness into the marvellous light of Jesus Christ. I've proved God in that way again and again and again.

I'll never forget the night that Zillah was baptised in the Holy Ghost. She laughed right into Pentecost. It was beautiful—beautiful! And it meant so much to me, because not only were we one—we were now one in spirit as well. I thank God that he gave Zillah to stand with me. She's been a true helpmeet, one that has never complained of the inconveniences of such ministry, one that has always been open-hearted and willing to encourage in this ministry. Thank God for her!

20

A Wider Ministry

But then, just over six years ago, I was in my study, and God spoke. You see, he's an ongoing God, isn't He? And God said, clear as clear, 'I want you to leave this church, and serve My Church.' What a tremendous call! 'I want you to leave this church, and serve My Church.' When I shared that with Zillah, again there was no argument. 'Then we must do it.' You'll appreciate: being in the church, we had a church house—we had no other house. Yet God said, 'I want you to come out of that church and serve My Church.' And that was in October.

And I told my deacons, I told my church that I was leaving. 'Where are you going?' 'I don't know.' 'What church are you going to?' 'I'm not going to a church.' And oh, you could see their thinking: 'He's away this time. Oh, he really has gone over the top this time.' And they said, 'Mr Hamilton, are you wise, walking out of this church with two children and a wife to support, and not knowing where you're going? Are you sure you're hearing from God?' Oh, the times that I got that poured into my ears: 'Are you sure you're hearing from God?' Friends, listen. If I didn't know God's voice, I would listen to theirs more than

I do. But I know the voice of God. Do you? I know the voice of God. 'My sheep hear My voice, and they follow Me.' Isn't that right? I know His voice. And I said, 'Look, I know that God has spoken'—although there was nothing there to go out to.

But God was working and God was moving, and in December Zillah's aunt died and left us the beautiful home that we're in today, in Yorkshire. You come and see it. God gave it.

I moved into Yorkshire not knowing, or knowing very little, about what God was going to do from that moment, not knowing very many people there. I did not advertise, I did not say, 'Look, I'm free to minister.' And friend, believe me, for the six years that I've spent serving His Church, my biggest problem is getting a holiday. Such is the faithfulness of God: such is the working of God. When He calls, He equips. And I've been to many parts of the world.

And I've shared with them what I share with you tonight: Jesus Christ is the answer to every need. Jesus Christ: Saviour, Healer, Baptiser, Coming King. And if He's not all these things to you tonight, then you have not moved into your inheritance. You have not possessed your possessions in Christ; you are at a loss tonight. But I'm believing God, that all who are in this gathering will come into their full possession in Christ, and you will come out and claim it now as we stand together in a moment. Whether it is for the Baptism in the Holy Spirit, whether it is for the healing of your afflictions, I want you to believe God tonight.

You have heard a testimony—and I'm sorry it's been so disjointed; it's very difficult to bring it all together in a few moments. But you have heard what God has done in my life. And the half has not been told. Much more could be told, for example of a time when He brought me into a situation where men were possessed and I stood alone and in the Name of Jesus commanded the very demons to come out of the people. And they came out, because there is power in the Name of Jesus Christ—power to set the captive free. There's power to heal and to deliver.

21

A Remarkable Vision

A Sick Church

One thing that has come to me over these past five years as God has thrust me out into different churches and fellowships is the sickness of the Church. You will appreciate that when I was in the pastoral work of one church my vision, my concern, was limited to that church, and rightly so— until God saw fit to send me further afield. But never in all my life as a Christian, as an evangelist, as a pastor, never in all my life did I believe or think that the Church was so sick and weak as I've seen it these five years. Never did I think that the Church was so broken and so ineffective and so weak, until one day in Germany after I had been counselling.

It was a day that I will never forget. And I believe that God allowed it for one purpose: that He might speak into my soul the word that He did speak. I don't know that I could have heard it had He not allowed certain things to happen that day. It seemed to me that every person, every Christian, who came into that office to be counselled was in a dreadful state—one seemed worse than the other, one problem seemed greater than the other. The whole day I heard of the sicknesses, of the uncleannesses, of the bondages, of the divisions, and so on and so on, that were in the lives of God's people.

And when I went into my room that night, I could not shake off the heaviness that was upon me. I still felt the uncleanness that had been poured into my ears. I felt that the fetters and the bondages that were shared in that private place of counselling were upon me—never before had I experienced this. But God wanted to speak into the situation. And He used these means to speak. And do you know that since that hour I have often thought, 'And yet, God, You carry the burden of Your Church. I had the burden of a few people. You carry the burden of Your Church daily upon Your heart.' It was only comparatively few people who came in that day, and yet it almost broke me. The burden, the weight of it, almost crushed my spirit. I went into that room, and I just fell on my face before God. I cried out, 'O God, can this be Your Church? can this be Your people? so weak, so unclean, so held in bondage and fetters, so divided, one man against another, one brother against another, and even in the Christian home, division?' And I cried out to God, not in a condemning tone of voice, but it was the cry of the heart, 'O God, can this really be Your Church? can this really be Your people that You said would be Your witnesses to the uttermost parts of the earth? can this be Your people that You said should be lights in the world?' Can you understand this cry? can you understand what I'm trying to say to you tonight? The question cried out of my heart, 'O God, can this really, can this really be the people that You have entrusted with the gospel of Your Son, Jesus Christ?'

The Inner Potential

And out of that cry came this answer. 'Tell My people that they have not yet fully realised the potential for God that lies within them.' Not to be given, not to be received in a future day. 'It is already there,' God said. 'Tell My people they have not yet fully realised the potential for God that is within them.'

Church, do you know what that potential is? That same Spirit that raised Jesus from the dead dwells, lives, abides within your heart tonight. Not another Spirit, not one like Him: the very same Spirit that raised Jesus Christ, the Son of God, from the dead, is dwelling within every believer, from the youngest, right to the oldest. It is the same Spirit that's in that young convert as is in that man who has walked these many years with His God.... God is saying, 'The very same Spirit that went right into hell itself and raised up Christ from the dead *dwells within My people.*' That is the potential: that is the power that dwells within every believer. And that is what Satan fears, and fears constantly. But you must recognise it: you must realise it.... In this five-feet-nothing the Spirit of the living God moves and works, and throbs within my very being! I can't understand it, I cannot comprehend it, but I tell you I live in the joy of it. I live in the liberty of it. I live in the strength of it every day: the same Spirit that raised my Jesus from the dead dwells within my life tonight. And that Spirit will always be there. Amen?

The Call of God

'Tell My people that that is the potential that is within them. And tell them of the call of God that is upon them.'

Do you hear that? The potential that's within you is only part of what God said. And you must know and understand the call of God that is upon you. 'As My Father sent Me, so I...*I will send you.*' Don't let that truth slide over. Let it come in. Let it come right into your being tonight. 'As My Father sent Me, so I will send you.' What a calling! And that call is on every life in this church tonight. He wants to send you. He wants you to go. As the Father sent Him, under that anointing of the Holy Ghost, He wants His Church to rise up and follow Him, under that same anointing that the Father gave Him.

Blessed be His Name! Oh, how He loves His Church! how He loves His people! how He gives! What more can He give, what more can He do, what more can He say to His Church, to get them up on to their feet and to go forward in His Name? Beloved, there is no more He can give, there is no more He can say, there is no more He can do. *It is done.* But when are we going to believe it? When are we going to walk in the liberty of it, in the power of it and in the might of it, that this generation may know that He lives, that they may know that He is Lord? If I ever stood before men and felt I had to apologise for my testimony and my trust, then I would go back right in behind that bar again. I would give up. But, beloved: there is no need to apologise. There is no need for any believer to be weak. There is no need for any believer to go out there and say, 'I cannot.' 'I can do all things through Christ Who strengthens me.' And He strengthens—I know that. He strengthens.

The Hands of Christ

And out of those words...came a beautiful vision...of His hands. And they were held out—the hands of God. And you were held there. And you were there, His people, held in His hands. The vision was glorious. Oh, I knew it, I knew it through His Word, that I am held in His hands: I knew it. I had known it through my day by day communion with Him, that I was held in His hands: I knew it. But I tell you, something happens to you when God lets you see it. And I rejoiced with exceeding joy as I saw His people held in His hands. The vision was glorious! Is it any wonder that

I rejoiced? Is it any wonder the burden lifted from my shoulders, as I saw His people, with all their problems, with all their needs, with all their afflictions—*they were held, in His hands!* blessed be His Name.

And then the vision changed. The hands began to move. And if you were held in His hands, and the hands were moving, there is no way you could be still. It would not be possible. And those hands began to move. I saw it. And I saw the Church of Jesus Christ being shaken by those hands. It wasn't the devil—don't give him the credit for that. It wasn't the devil that was shaking the Church; it was God, God Himself, shaking His people. And how we need to be shaken, don't we? How we need to be shaken by those mighty hands. And they were moving. And I can only describe it to you as I saw it in the vision: as if in a great big cement mixer, the Church was being thrown all over the place, this way and that way. Men were going all over the place, and women too—the whole Church. Not one person was in the same place. Every person was being moved.

But when the hands stopped, when the hands stood still...every man, every woman, every boy and every girl was in the right place; not one life, not one member of that Church was out of place. Every one was in the right place at the right time with the right words to the right people. That is the desire of God for His people. And He will not rest, and He will not be silent, until that vision is totally completed. And you and I know that there's a lot of work to be done to bring that vision to fulfilment. I've never known the Church to be so divided. I've never known men to be so vague as to what God's will is for their lives. I've never heard such paltry excuses as to why certain things are being done in the Church. And, beloved, there is no call of God on some men's lives. They have been sent by men and not by God. And in that vision I saw men come out of the pulpit and into the pew. They should never have been in the pulpit in the first place: God never put them there. Do you understand this? And I saw some in the pew standing in the pulpit: that's where God wanted them to be, declaring His word. I saw Sunday School teachers come out of the Sunday School; they should never have been there in the first place: God never sent them there. They were only there because nobody else was doing it. Do you get the picture tonight? Can you see the great concern of God for His people? Can you see what God is saying to His Church? that men and women are teaching children His Word for no other reason than that nobody else is doing it. There is no call of God on them. And I don't care if you just give out the hymnbooks and welcome people to come in: if that's where God wants you to be, then that is where God will bless you, and make you a blessing. And that is the only place you've a right to ask His help. We have no right, no right at all ever to ask God to help us in any work we are doing unless we know absolutely and fully that 'that is the call of God on my life.'

Knowing the Score

If I were to start from the front row right through this congregation, and ask you a very simple question, you would be amazed and astounded at the answers I would receive to this one question from this one church. It's a very simple question: Do you know the will of God for your life? And right through the church, the variety of answers that I would get from a people who are redeemed by the Blood of Christ, who are baptised in the Holy Ghost, and who have sat under anointed ministry, would astound you...do you hear me? How many in this church tonight could stand up and declare without a moment's hesitation, 'I know that I am where I am, because God has called me here. This is the place of His appointing for my life'—how many could say that? I think only a very small section in this church could say that. I think the rest would be so vague, and it would be, 'Well, I *hope* I'm doing what's right, I *would like* to know the will of God, I'm *praying* about it....' And this is His people; these are His instruments; these are His witnesses to this generation and whatever generation might follow.

And He wants His people to know that He has a plan, He has a purpose, He has a place, He has a work that only they can do. And, beloved, I want to say to you tonight: do not rest and do not be satisfied until you know it—without a shade of doubt you can say before God and before men, 'I am standing in the will of God.' Does He not deserve this? is He not worthy of this? that you should know His calling, that He has paid the fullest price that you might walk in the centre of His will? Surely tonight He deserves that, that we should not be a people so vague, so uncertain, so scattered, running hither and thither, and not really knowing, 'Is this His place? is this His plan? is this His purpose?' Surely the God Who saved you, and the God Who has promised to meet your every need, surely He has a place and a plan for your life? He does not want you to run forever hither and thither not really knowing His will for your life.

And it's only in that place, I believe, that you will see the affliction of His people, that you will know the sorrows of His people, that you will hear the cry of His people, and you will be able under Him to deliver His people out of bondage, out of fetters, and serve Him and bring glory to His Name. That is His call. That is His desire.

Do you see what God is saying? that potential that's within you? He may not call you across the sea; He might just call you across the street—but you'll know it. Don't ever limit the call of God to a call to the mission field. It can be that, but not only that. It's knowing that you're in the right place at the right time with the right word to the right people. That is the call of God. And I believe in my heart that when that is fulfilled, the church will walk in revival.

The Cry of His People

And as the vision was given, and as I waited in His presence, I realised that God was going to do something new in my life, at that moment. The knowledge was there, that God had not finished yet. And out of that experience of the vision that God gave, and the word that He gave to give to His people, God allowed me to hear the cry of His people, in that room. I heard the cry of the Church. I heard it. I was like water poured out. I can't describe it to you; it's indescribable.

And God said, 'Have you heard this? have you heard this cry?'

I said, 'Yes, Lord.'

'And what will you do about this cry?'

And there is no sham, and there is no hypocrisy escapes your lips in such an encounter with God as that was. And I said, 'O God, there is nothing I can do about it. Nothing.' And God said, 'That is right. There is nothing *you* can do about it. But rise, stand on your feet, and go.'

Now this would be about four o'clock or five o'clock in the morning. And I did not know a word of German; I still don't know any German. I said, 'O Lord, go where?' And no answer came. Now there was only one door in the room, and I went through that door.

And as I went into the next room, there was a group of young people on their knees before God, praying. One stood up, and I knew he was not praying. Although I did not know German, I knew he was not praying. I knew he was prophesying. After it was over, I went right up to this young man and said, 'Frank, tell me, were you prophesying?' He said, 'Yes, I was.' 'Please share that prophecy with me.' And he shared it. I will not give you the full prophecy; I'll only share this with you, that in that prophecy came these words that you've heard tonight: 'I have seen the

194

affliction of My people, I know the sorrows of My people, I have heard the cry of My people, and I have come down to deliver My people. Come now, and I will send you.'

And I knew in that hour that was God's call on my life. I knew it. I didn't want it. I don't know if I want it even yet. But I knew, when that young fellow spoke these words, that God wanted me to hear them. And from that place I went out knowing that that word would be fulfilled as I walk before God. I've heard that cry. I've heard it again and again and again.

I hear it tonight, in this church: the cry of the afflictions of men, the cry of bondage, the sorrows that are in so many people tonight, the afflictions of the soul and of the body, the fetters that bind you, the bondages that hold you captive. And God said, 'I have seen them.' The cry, the cry that comes from a heart that can't even make it audible, it's so deep. You understand it, don't you, tonight, in this place, that all over this gathering there are men, there are women here, and there's a cry. It cannot be audible: it's so deep. God said, 'I've heard it. I've heard it. I see that spirit that's broken. I see that sorrow that is unbearable. I know your afflictions. And I have come down to deliver you.' We're going to go right into that word now. We've not come just to listen to a sermon. This word is going to be manifest to you tonight; He says, 'Look, I've seen your afflictions.'

Appendix

The Gift of Knowledge in Operation

[The tapes from which Mr Hamilton's testimony has been transcribed cover three services and excerpts from the appeals made at the end of each are included here. The services were of the outreach type and many responded and received ministry. The operation of the gift of knowledge brings a real sense of the presence of God, with fear for the hard of heart and hope for the penitent. Suddenly the New Testament springs into life and the works of God are manifestly wrought before men.].

Excerpts from first appeal

God is speaking to someone here tonight. I don't say that just to sound clever at the end of a testimony; I say it because I believe it. And that's what I want to share with you before I hand back to Mr Black. There are many, many people whose lives are full of *fear*. Many, many people who are depressed, insecure, lonely, not only outside this building but, believe me, right here in this City Hall. There are many like that tonight in this place. And there are even some in this hall who have tried suicide. And God has brought you to this very moment, that you might know, as you have never known before, that He came to give life, and life more abundant; He came to set you free from every bondage and to break every fetter that's in your life.

And in a moment I'm going to ask you to respond to what God has given me for this evening. And the one thing that is stronger than all the others is the knowledge of *the fear of man* in His Church. Do you hear me? I am speaking now to God's people. There are many in this gathering who are saved, who are baptised in the Holy Spirit, but who suffer from fear. God tonight will break that fetter of fear that has held you captive for many years. I'm going to ask people once on this matter—only once. Christian, you know what I'm saying is from God, because you know that's exactly where you are tonight. You've got a testimony, and you'd love to give it, and you want to give it, but the fear of man seals your lips in testimony. And time and time again you've stood before men and you've known that you should speak for your Lord, but the fear of man has held you silent. I tell you, that's a fearful bondage for any Christian to be in. But I know tonight that God reveals to heal. Will you remember that? He reveals to heal. He does not reveal to fill my mind with people's problems. He reveals to heal and to set free from that particular bondage or fetter that you're in. If you know that I have described your condition—that you have a testimony, but it's not given because of the fear of others —I would like you simply to stand to your feet. And all I'm going to do is pray that God will break that fetter of fear in your life, and you will know that the bondage has gone. Will you do it now?...Many, many more should be standing to their feet in this hall. [About forty were standing.—H.B.B.] 'And you shall know the truth, and the truth shall make you free.' The word of God to you who are standing has already been quoted: 'I have not given you the spirit of fear, but of love and of a sound mind and of power'...I want all who stood to know that that fetter is broken, completely broken. And you shall be His witnesses, and you shall be bold witnesses, for Jesus Christ. And I tell you, on the authority of His Word, He will make you true disciples of Jesus Christ, where no fear or fetter will ever hold you captive again. That's why He came, to destroy the works of the devil. And they are destroyed tonight. The fear of man brings a snare. But oh, that the Church of Jesus Christ would rise up in this hour and go forward without fear or fetter to serve Him and declare that He is Lord.

Many who are here are afflicted with *depression*. Will you stand to your feet? Would you come forward and we'll pray for you.... There are some men who should be coming forward who are depressive...we'll wait a moment longer ...God makes no mistakes. This is not just speaking from the top of my mind. This is, as Mr Black said, the word of knowledge. There are men here, and you too are afflicted by depression.... There's a man at the back there—yes, right, just come forward. Yes, you too. For this purpose Jesus came, to destroy the works of the devil. And He'll fill your mouth with laughter, and the joy of the Lord shall be your strength. I want those of you who are in the congregation not to be spectators, please. Be participators: pray—pray. I tell you, there's a real battle here tonight. But Jesus is Victor...

Such a *spirit of uncleanness*...can I just say that again? There is such a spirit of uncleanness throughout the Church. And I believe that we need to repent of this uncleanness before God. I'm not going to ask you to come to the front; I'm just going to ask you to stand to your feet, if you know that that is a bondage in your life. Will you stand to your feet now? Let Jesus set you free tonight; let the Blood of Christ cleanse you again tonight. It has become a fearful bondage, that uncleanness within your life. Many, many more should be standing. God wants to cleanse His people,

God wants to purify His Church. And these unclean habits, these unclean thoughts and desires...God is not pleased. He wants to set you free; He wants to deliver you and make you clean again. We're going to wait another moment. But oh, I see many men who're still sitting who should stand. Yes, away at the back there—over at the very back there there are people who should be standing. That's right, that's right. Don't wait for hands to be laid upon you. Just repent, repent, and seek God tonight for that cleansing. And He will cleanse you; He will set you free. Thank You, Father. [Congregation is singing, 'Spirit of the Living God.'] The bondage breaks—the bondage breaks—the bondage breaks, through the power of the Blood of Jesus. Yes, you're free; it's broken. He breaks every fetter: believe it—He's doing it now, yes, He is. That's the Spirit of God that's upon you. You don't need the hands of men: His hand is there, His Spirit is there, the Blood of Christ is there, cleansing, cleansing. Thank You, Father.

I want those of you who are standing to know: the vision is glorious. The Blood of Christ has cleansed, and the power that's in the Name of Christ has broken that bondage of uncleanness. You are clean through the Blood and through the word of Jesus Christ. Oh, praise Him, that He set you free from that uncleanness, that you are made clean by the Blood of Christ, that that fetter falls at His feet tonight, and you rise up clean and made whole in the Name of Jesus. Thank You, Father...thank You, Lord.

As I was travelling in the car today God revealed something to me; I'm sure He meant me to share it tonight. It's about a *marriage* that is *broken*; not broken by law, but broken under that roof. And both of you are here tonight. You live apart. Both of you are Christians, but your marriage is broken. And God showed me very clearly He's going to heal that marriage: He's going to heal it. And I know that that man and that woman are in here tonight. God showed it very clearly. I would like you to come to the front, just come forward, and believe God is going to heal that marriage. Thank You, Father. Thank You, Jesus. Oh, thank You, Lord....

The revelation has only been given me for one couple, but God is greater than the revelation. It may be that there are others here tonight and you know that your marriage needs healing. Will you come forward, and we'll pray for you. Will you do it now? Thank you...yes, thank You, Father.

'Now is the accepted time. Now is *the day of salvation*.' And it could be tonight there are people in this gathering who have not yet tasted of that salvation, you know nothing of the joy of the forgiveness of sins through the Blood of Christ. Tonight we would like you to respond to the call of God, to come and put your trust in Him, that you might know as we know that Christ is the answer. You don't have to be an alcoholic. You don't have to be depressive, suicidal. You don't have to have any of the things that were in my life. But the Bible clearly teaches that all have sinned, all have come short of the glory of God. There is none righteous, not one. And so tonight we want to give you this opportunity. If through the testimony, or through others who have witnessed to you, you know in your heart you need to get right with God, you need to come and put your trust in Him: we want you to come forward, right at this moment. By coming forward you're saying, 'I want to become a Christian, I want Jesus Christ to come into my life. I want to know His salvation.' Will you do that now— will you come forward? Remember: 'Today if you hear His voice, do not harden your heart.' Oh, I know the struggle, I know it; I know the fear that can come in at such an appeal as this. But I tell you, if you will just take that step, God will break that fear and you will know the joy of sins forgiven and peace with God.

'Father, known to you are all men. And we thank You, You are not willing that any should perish, but all should have eternal life. And so, Father, we ask that when our voice is silent, You will speak on to those in this gathering who know You not as Saviour. Lord, do not let them go. Continue to strive, continue to convict and convince and convert, that they might know that Your salvation is real, O God, that they might go from this place knowing that they are born again of Your Spirit. Thank You for all that You have given us; thank You, O God, for the richness of Your presence in this place. Thank You for the deep moving of Your Spirit upon hearts. And we pray that You will go on to work, You will go on to move, You'll go on, O God, to speak to all our hearts. Father, bring us quickly to the place of Your appointing. Let not this be an abortive time; but let this meeting bring forth life, and let it bring forth testimonies to the glory and to the praise of Your great Name. For You are worthy, O Lord. And for this we give You praise, in Jesus' Name. Amen, Amen.

Excerpts from second appeal

There's someone over here and you are under terrible *afflictions*, terrible afflictions. And God says, 'I've seen every one of them.' And there is over that life severe temptation to give up and to give in because of the enormity of that affliction. Will you stand to your feet—on this side here?... 'I've seen your afflictions, I've seen them, and I will deliver you.' Will you believe His word tonight—'I will deliver you'? That burden that's on you tonight, my brother—it will not crush you. He will lift it—He will lift its weight....

Oh the cry! the cry from people in this church tonight! I'm going to ask you just to do one thing. You know that cry that is there in your heart. Never have you expressed it.

Never have you shared it. It is a cry that is in you. But God wants you to express it tonight. Will you just stand to your feet, all of you, who know that this word is for you tonight: 'I have seen your afflictions, I know your sorrows, I have heard your cry, and I have come down to deliver you out of these afflictions, out of these bondages, out of these fetters' .... Those who know tonight that they need this word to be fulfilled and made manifest through them—will you stand to your feet?... 'I am come down to deliver.'

Bondage to alcohol—God will set you gloriously free tonight from its power. Don't sit there in your bondage and your fetters—Jesus' word is given tonight: 'I will set you free.'

And now I'm going to put a very straight question to all who are here tonight. There are at least thirty to forty people who have been praying earnestly for *the will of God to be made known* to them. It's not yet known, but oh, there's been a cry in your heart, a longing, 'O God, what would you have me to do?' Would you stand to your feet tonight? 'As my Father sent me, so I will send you.'

There's *a man* here tonight *like Jonah*. God called you many years ago, and you ran away from that call. But tonight God has hemmed you in again to that call. And you're here tonight and God has spoken again to you. And that door is still open. God has kept that door open for you, but He wants you to go through that door. Would you just like to stand to your feet now? A door is opened, that no man can shut...and you will go through that door, and through that door you will find God's abundance waiting, for you will lack nothing as you go out in His will, and He shall make you that servant, the ordained person that you ought to be. And no fear or fetter will bind you, but with an assurance and a confidence you will go forth in His Name, and you will bring praise and honour and glory unto Him. The door is still open, and you will go through it. No man,

no power, will shut that door. Blessed be His Name....
Thank you, Father; thank you, Lord....

There are many, many people to whom God has given
gifts of the Spirit. But the *gifts* are *lying dormant;* they are
not being used as He wants them to be used. They are not
being manifested as He longs to have them manifest through
His Church. And I believe that it is right to ask you to come
again to God and say, 'Lord, I want these gifts stirred up
within me, that they may come forth.' Whatever the gift
that God has given, it was never intended to lie dormant
within you. It was that it might be manifest through you to
the building up of His Church and to the benefit of His
people. I believe that there are many in this church who
have gifts which are not being used. The opportunities are
there, and the needs are there for these gifts to be manifest,
but they are not coming forth. Now, I don't know the
reasons for that, but I do know that they are lying there
dormant within you. I want you to ask God to stir up these
gifts that are within you, to His praise and to His glory.

'O God, we pray that You will meet with Your people
now, and, Lord, that by the Holy Spirit You will stir up
these gifts that are within them, that the ministry shall come
forth, anointed by the Holy Spirit; that the gifts shall be
sharpened daily under Your hand, and that they shall be
manifest to the praise and to the honour and to the glory of
Your great Name. O God, let this be now, we pray. Let
there be a stirring within these who stand before You now.
Let it come, Lord. Let that prophecy come, let that tongue
come, let that gift come forth. O God, unto You, unto You,
Lord, shall the glory and the praise be given. For You and
You alone are worthy to receive it.'

Yes, these gifts are being stirred up; I sense in many here
tonight that the gifts of God are being stirred within you.
And oh, hallelujah, the power of God is being made manifest
through you now.

There is *healing* for someone here tonight. God is healing already. The power of God is present to heal in this gathering. There is someone being healed; I sense a healing now. Will you stand to your feet if you know that God has touched you in healing now? There's someone over here ...yes.... Thank You, Lord Jesus; thank You, Father, in Jesus' Name.

[*Mr Black's comments on the occasion:* I would like to explain, in case there are some who don't really understand the operation of the word of knowledge, that in the early part of the service you heard Mr. Hamilton preach under anointing; the Holy Spirit was upon Him as he preached. And there is a sense in which, when a man is preaching under unction, there is knowledge in a general sense in operation. But there came later in the service a time when the Holy Spirit was impressing upon Mr. Hamilton particular needs that lay within the congregation, particular conditions of particular individuals. And when that begins to operate, the servant of God may have a clear revelation of a totally hidden condition that nobody knows anything about except the person concerned and God. That can be revealed, and the person in that condition can also be identified. And God in great graciousness draws near, and He lets a man or a woman know that they are known of God, and in being known of God they are loved of God, and that God is desirous of healing the condition that is causing the difficulty. He draws near not just to expose a person as it were in front of a company, but to reach down into the deep need of the human heart, and to set the man or the woman free. God is exceedingly gracious in the way in which He operates. And my spirit is aglow tonight. I believe that the living God has walked in the midst of us. The Lord Jesus Christ has been here. And there are lives, I believe, that will have been very deeply changed. To God be the glory.

Excerpts from third appeal

As I came into this hall tonight, there were just three things that God showed me; and those three things I will share with you. And as I speak these things out and you relate to them, I would ask you to respond in a very simple way. Just stand to your feet if what you're saying is, 'Yes, that's me. That word is for me.' And I'll tell you why I'm asking you to do that. You're responding to the revelation of God over your life. And God reveals to heal.

God showed me very clearly even as we stood and sang, 'He is Lord,' that it is true of many people in this gathering that it's by lip only that they sing. Do you hear that? It's by lip, only, they sing such words. There are *backsliders* here tonight. Now I don't mean by backsliding you're running to the dance, you're standing behind the bar, and you're going to discos, and all these things. Friend, there is a backsliding that is deeper than that: a backsliding that goes on under the sound of His Word every week, a backsliding that goes on under the voice of the preacher telling you the good news that Jesus loves you, and yet some of you here in this gathering sit, week after week, month after month, year after year, and your heart is far from Him. Tonight God is saying, 'I want you to come back. I want you to arise, as the Prodigal did, and say, "I will go to my Father and I will say, I have sinned against Heaven and before you"' ....

Now there are others that I want to come right down to the front, not just to stand, but to come forward because I want to minister to those of you tonight who can relate to the second revelation that God has given. And believe me, this is going to take courage. But God will give the courage to do it. There are four people—four who are harbouring *resentment* in their hearts, deep resentment.... And that resentment is eating like a cancer in their life....

Shall we just stand to our feet. You know, throughout the

church, there comes a *murmuring*, a *complaining*, a *criticising*. And that grieves the Holy Spirit. It ties the hands of God. And the enemy laughs as he looks upon a people redeemed by the Blood of Christ, baptised in the Holy Ghost, hearing the anointed Word; and yet going out with murmurings and criticism. I want you to be real tonight, friends. If you're not real before God now, then don't expect God to be real to you. It's only as you respond, it's only as you are real before God, that you will know that work of God manifest in your life. And I want you... those who have murmured, those who have complained against His work, criticised His servants—it's a big thing I'm asking; but it's a big God that you're going to stand before—will you come to the front now and say, 'Father, forgive me, that my tongue has spoken against Your anointed.'

NOTE TO READERS

If you would like to enquire further about issues raised in this book or if you feel that the author could be of help, you are invited to write to him at 27 Denholm Street, Greenock, PA16 8RH, Scotland, or telephone 0475 87432.

It may also be of interest to know that the author is normally involved in five conferences in Scotland each year—New Year, Easter, July, August and October. Friends gather from many parts of Britain. An open invitation is extended to all and particularly to those interested in the Baptism in the Holy Spirit and related themes. Details will be provided on enquiry.

By the same author

Reflections on the Baptism in the Holy Spirit

The Baptism in the Holy Spirit

- Is it something that happens to us all at conversion, or is it a later and separate experience?
- Should people tarry for it?
- Is it the same as sanctification?
- Do tongues always come with it?
- What about men like Spurgeon and Finney? Did they have this experience?

This book honestly faces many of the problems that the Baptism in the Spirit has raised in the minds of so many in our day. The fact that tens of millions of people now claim to have had this experience, which they describe as similar to what happened to the early disciples on the day of Pentecost, makes the book both topical and relevant.

Published in December 1987, the book has proved very popular and is likely to be used as a textbook on the subject.

£2.25 UK   128pp

By the same author

Reflections on the Gifts of the Spirit

This book speaks of...
- the wonderful operation of the gift of knowledge
- demon exorcism
- miracles of many kinds

Examples are largely drawn from the present day and fall within the personal experience of the author, or of people close to him. Intriguing questions are raised...
- Do demons still speak through human lips?
- Can people receive instantaneous healing?
- Is the future sometimes accurately revealed to God's servants?
- Is angelic ministry real and does it happen today?
- Finally does an ex-Headmaster of a large secondary school, qualified in History (a subject which so often breeds sceptics) believe all these things?

This book contains a number of unusual insights on the gifts in general and on healing, miracles and exorcism in particular.

£2.75   192pp

By the same author

Reflections on a Song of Love

(A Commentary on 1 Corinthians 13)

First Corinthians Thirteen has a beauty which has enthralled readers through the ages. It highlights Love and reveals attributes of Christ Himself. It has, however, often been used by opponents at Pentecostal doctrine—quite wrongly, the author maintains. He raises intriguing questions...

- 'Whether there be tongues, they shall cease': did this happen with the close of the canon of Scripture?
- Did knowledge cease at the same time? Will knowledge ever cease in this life, and what will replace it in Heaven?
- When Paul became a man he 'put away childish things.' Did this not include tongues?
- Do Christians generally attain the level of Love taught here, and do they display it in their attitudes to each other, as, for example, when these doctrines deeply divide them?

While the main part of this book gives a wonderful description of Christ and the quality of His Love, these controversial issues are not overlooked. Published in April 1988, this highly original commentary on 1 Corinthians 13 has attracted considerable attention.

£1.25   64pp

By the same author

A Trumpet Call
To Women

Is it true that in the Old Testament there were:

Prophetesses?
A Woman Judge?
A Queen (in her own right)?

and in the New Testament:

Prophetesses?   Women Apostles?
Women Teachers?   Women Elders?
Women Evangelists?   Women Deacons?

- What did Paul mean when He taught that in the Church there is neither male nor female?
- And was what the Maréchale said true, 'There is no sex in soul'?
- And are all the spiritual functions which are open to men equally open to women?
- Or should women be in a role subject to men?

This is a highly original piece of writing. The author deals in a Biblical way with the question of women ministry. Unlike those who base their case on 'cultural relativism', Mr Black finds his support in the writings of Paul himself. He produces what to many will be an unexpectedly powerful and persuasive case for the ministry of women.

This is a valuable contribution to the current debate.

Published in 1988, this thoughtful and original work has attracted wide attention.

£2.50   152pp

By the same author

Consider Him

(Twelve Qualities of Christ)

Like a man gazing into a fathomless pool the author has looked into the infinite deeps of Christ. As the colours of a glorious sky are reflected in ever changing light so the radiance of Heaven is reflected in the soul of Christ. We see glory change to glory as we behold His face.

What are the qualities which appear as in a kaleidoscope?

- Peace and Serenity
- Purity and Tranquillity
- Love and Compassion
- Strength and Courage
- Self-effacement and God-centredness
- Power and Glory

The subjects are not treated in a milk and water way. At times the writing cuts like a knife and lays bare our very souls. Our loyalty and commitment are deeply challenged as we are measured, not by our own faulty standards but by His perfection nor are we expected to stop at intellectual instruction. Change is demanded and expected.

This recently published book should appeal to Christians interested in both sound doctrine and a devotional approach to God.

£2.25

By the same author

The Clash of Tongues

(A Commentary on 1 Corinthians 14)

This work deals not only with the regulation of gifts of the Spirit and their relevance for today but also with some of the deeper principles underlying their use. It raises fundamental questions which are sometimes overlooked:

- How can an individual be edified through speaking something which he cannot understand?
- What is the point of speaking in this way when the hearers do not understand either?
- Is there a spiritual means of communication between the human spirit and God which by-passes the intellect but still yields benefit?
- Why did Paul have to make regulations at all? If the gifts are Gifts of the Spirit, how can error creep into their use?
- Do the regulations not clash with the direct unctioning of the Spirit upon an individual?
- Tongues, according to verse 2 of 1 Corinthians 14, are Godward. Why then is interpretation in modern times so often manward? Surely if God is addressed in one, He will be addressed in the other. Is there Scriptural justification for present-day practice?
- Was there a difference between the tongues of Acts 2, which were understood by foreigners and the 'tongues' of 1 Corinthians 14 which 'no man' understood?

These and other points are dealt with as they arise in the text, and it is hoped that both spiritual and intellectual benefit may be derived from the perusal of the solutions offered.

Due for later publication this book, while of general interest, is expected to appeal particularly to serious students of the New Testament.

£2.50

BOOK ORDERS

The books advertised on the previous pages are being made available to Christian booksellers throughout the country, but if you have any difficulty in obtaining your supply, you may order directly from New Dawn Books, c/o 27 Denholm Street, Greenock, Scotland, PA16 8RH.

·········· ORDER FORM ··········

Please send me the books indicated below:

Quantity	Title	Price
	Reflections on the Baptism in the Holy Spirit	£2.25
	Reflections on the Gifts of the Spirit	£2.75
	Reflections on a Song of Love (A commentary on 1 Cor 13)	£1.25
	A Trumpet Call to Women	£2.50
	Consider Him (Twelve Qualities of Christ)	£2.25
	Battle for the Body	£2.95
	The Clash of Tongues with Glimpses of Revival	£2.50

Signature . . . .

Address . . . .

. . . .

When ordering please send purchase price plus 30p per book to help cover the cost of postage and packaging.